Seven Secrets for Negotiating with **Government**

Also by Jeswald W. Salacuse:

Leading Leaders: How to Manage Smart, Talented, Rich, and Powerful People

The Global Negotiator: Making, Managing, and Mending Deals around the World in the Twenty-First Century

The Wise Advisor: What Every Professional Should Know about Consulting and Counseling

Making Global Deals: Negotiating in the International Market Place

The Art of Advice: How to Give It and How to Take It

International Business Planning: Law and Taxation (with W.P. Streng, six volumes)

Social Legislation in the Contemporary Middle East (co-editor with L. Michalak)

An Introduction to Law in French-Speaking Africa: North Africa

An Introduction to Law in French-Speaking Africa: Africa South of the Sahara

Nigerian Family Law (with A. B. Kasunmu)

Seven Secrets for Negotiating with **Government**

How to Deal with Local, State, National, or Foreign Governments – and Come Out Ahead

Jeswald W. Salacuse

AMACOM

American Management Association
New York • Atlanta • Brussels • Chicago • Mexico City • San Francisco
Shanghai • Tokyo • Toronto • Washington, D.C.

Special discounts on bulk quantities of AMACOM books are available to corporations, professional associations, and other organizations. For details, contact Special Sales Department, AMACOM, a division of American Management Association, 1601 Broadway, New York, NY 10019.
Tel.: 212-903-8316 Fax: 212-903-8083
E-mail: specialsls@amanet.org
Website: www.amacombooks.org/go/specialsales
To view all AMACOM titles go to: www.amacombooks.org

This publication is designed to provide accurate and authoritative information in regard to the subject matter covered. It is sold with the understanding that the publisher is not engaged in rendering legal, accounting, or other professional service. If legal advice or other expert assistance is required, the services of a competent professional person should be sought.

Library of Congress Cataloging-in-Publication Data

Salacuse, Jeswald W.
  Seven secrets for negotiating with government : how to deal with local, state, national, or foreign governments—and come out ahead / Jeswald W. Salacuse.
    p. cm.
  Includes bibliographical references and index.
  ISBN-13: 978-0-8144-0908-4
  ISBN-10: 0-8144-0908-3
  1. Negotiation in business. 2. Business and politics. I. Title.

HD58.6.S257 2008
658.4'052—dc22   2007022411

© 2008 Jeswald W. Salacuse.
All rights reserved.
Printed in the United States of America.

This publication may not be reproduced,
stored in a retrieval system,
or transmitted in whole or in part,
in any form or by any means, electronic,
mechanical, photocopying, recording, or otherwise,
without the prior written permission of AMACOM,
a division of American Management Association,
1601 Broadway, New York, NY 10019.

Printing number

10 9 8 7 6 5 4 3 2 1

For Anna and Miles

Contents

Preface		ix
Chapter 1.	The Many Ways of Negotiating with Governments	1
Chapter 2.	Governments Feel Different: How Negotiating with a Government Differs from Negotiating with Anybody Else	21
Chapter 3.	Getting Ready to Negotiate with a Government	46
Chapter 4.	The Myth of the Monolith: How Government Organization Affects Negotiations	72
Chapter 5.	The Political Imperative: The Special Nature of Government Interests and How They Affect Negotiations	101
Chapter 6.	Power Tools for Influencing Government Decisions	118
Chapter 7.	Getting a Little Help from Your Friends: Using Third Parties in Government Negotiations	145
Chapter 8.	The Deal Is Never Done: Renegotiating Government Agreements	161

Chapter 9. On the Manner of Negotiating with Governments: Some Final Advice	193
Notes	199
Index	205

Preface

The purpose of this book is to help you succeed in your dealings with governments. It is based on three fundamental propositions. First, the primary method for individuals and organizations to deal with governments is negotiation. Second, negotiations with governments are different from other kinds of negotiations. Third, despite vast differences in cultures and political systems, all governments—local, state, national, and foreign—perceive and conduct negotiations in similar ways. This book takes the view that negotiating with governments, a vital and virtually constant task for most organizations and many individuals today, constitutes a distinct type of negotiation that demands special skills, techniques, and strategies.

A government has been defined as an institution having a monopoly over the use of force in a society. That monopoly gives it a position of power in any negotiation that no private company or individual ever has. Indeed, many government officials who deal with private individuals and organizations would deny that what they do is "negotiation." According to them, governments decide, direct, or authorize; they don't negotiate. A fundamental challenge in dealing with any government therefore is how to overcome this real or perceived imbalance of power at the bargaining table. Whereas discussions of negotiation in many books and articles presuppose a model of two individuals with equal bargaining power, that model hardly ever exists in negotiations with governments.

Seven Secrets for Negotiating with Government: How to Deal with Local, State, National, or Foreign Governments—And Come Out Ahead is designed to help individuals and organizations prepare for, meet, and succeed at the very special challenges of negotiating with governments at all levels. In particular, it will show you how to cope with the greater power you inevitably face on the other side of the negotiating table whenever you have to deal with a government. Toward that end, it presents seven power tools that can level the playing field and enable you to obtain your goals in government negotiations.

Drawing on my research, including interviews with skilled negotiators working in a variety of contexts, and my own thirty years of experience dealing with governments throughout the world, this book explains the factors influencing government negotiating behavior and then offers techniques that organizations and individuals can use to succeed in those negotiations. Applying the insights and approaches of "interest-based negotiation" developed at the Harvard Program on Negotiation in which I have participated as a faculty member for nearly twenty years, as well as established methods of diplomacy that governments use in dealing with one another, I explain how to understand and analyze the often hidden interests driving government negotiators—and, most important, how to use that knowledge to achieve your goals.

I believe that *Seven Secrets for Negotiating with Government* is a unique work that fills an important void. No other book exists that is devoted exclusively and comprehensively to the techniques of negotiating with governments at all levels, both in the United States and abroad. While portions of some works discuss the problems of negotiating with specific governments, this book presents a comprehensive approach to governmental negotiations that you can apply in Peoria or Prague with a wide array of government agencies and departments in diverse settings, from a village clerk's office to a presidential mansion.

Seven Secrets for Negotiating with Government is the product of three decades of experience, conversation, and study. I am grateful to the many negotiators, scholars, and government officials who have shared their thoughts with me during that time on the nature and challenges of government negotiations. In that connection, I particularly want to thank my colleagues at the Fletcher School of Law and Diplomacy, Tufts University, and the Program on Negotiation at Harvard Law School for the insights that they have provided me on this topic. I am also indebted to Susan Powers, who assisted with the research for this book, and Donna Booth Salacuse, who once again brought her superb editorial skills and judgment to improving the manuscript.

Seven Secrets for Negotiating with **Government**

• CHAPTER ONE •

The Many Ways of Negotiating with Governments

"You can't fight city hall."

—ANONYMOUS

You may not be able to fight city hall, but you certainly can negotiate with it. In fact, short of successful armed insurrection, the only way any individual or company can deal effectively with any government—local, state, national, or foreign—is through negotiation. If it's true, as Edmund Burke has said, that "government is a contrivance of human wisdom to provide for human needs," it is also true that governments do not necessarily provide for your needs automatically. You have to negotiate to get them.

The Scope of Dealings with Governments

Dealings with governments by individuals and organizations cover a wide variety of participants, a multiplicity of purposes, and a broad array of processes. In this first chapter, we examine the scope of dealing with governments by focusing on three key elements: participants, purposes, and processes. They are the conceptual building blocks for analyzing and thinking about any kind of interaction with a government.

1

Participants in Dealings with Governments

Although governments and governmental units deal with each other constantly, the focus of this book is how individuals and non-governmental organizations can best deal with governments to get what they want. In those kinds of interactions, there are potentially three participants: a governmental unit; an individual or organization; and the public. Let's examine the special characteristics of each one.

Governments as Participants

Any time you have to deal with a government, you are actually negotiating with a governmental unit, rather than an entire government, and in particular, with individuals within that unit. Governmental units take many forms and have many names: department, agency, board, council, court, legislature, or commission, to list just a few. They are agents of governmental power, and the power they exercise may be legislative (to the extent that they make laws, regulations, or rules), executive (to the extent that they apply laws, regulations, and rules to individuals and organizations), or judicial (to the extent that they judge disputes concerning these laws, regulations, and rules and their application). In the United States alone in 2005, there were some 88,000 federal, state, and local governmental units employing approximately 19 million people, not to mention the countless governmental entities existing in the 192 other sovereign states of the world. Consequently, unless you are a hermit in the wilderness, you are bound to have to deal with one of them at some time or other.

Governments as Ghost Participants at the Negotiating Table

Even when a government entity is not physically present at the negotiating table, it may be lurking in the wings as a "ghost negotiator" that has a powerful influence on the parties who are actually engaged in face-to-face negotiations. For example, any deal you make with a private defense contractor will almost always require

U.S. government approval, and in most foreign countries any sizable transaction at all needs a nod from the governing authorities. So even if you are not negotiating directly with a government in those situations, you still will eventually have to deal with one or more governmental units if you hope to make the transaction you want. In any significant negotiation, you should always ask two important questions:

1. To what extent does a government have an actual or potential interest in this deal?
2. How might that government intervene in the negotiation or the resulting transaction to protect that interest?

Individuals and Organizations as Participants

All of us have to deal with governmental units at one time or other. Some of us do it only occasionally. Others do it every day. We deal with governments in our individual capacity and we deal with them in our capacity as representatives of the companies and organization that we work for. Whether we are seeking a building permit from our local zoning board to put an addition on our house, an authorization from the state to open a new charter school, or a contract to sell software to the U.S. Defense Department, we have to negotiate with some government agency to get what we want.

If you are in business, dealing with local, state, federal, and even foreign regulators can be a constant task requiring you to reach agreement with government agencies as diverse as the New York City Department of Planning, the California Air Resources Board, the U.S. Environmental Protection Agency, and even the European Union's Competition Directorate General, to name just a few. And if you want to undertake a really big project or transaction, you normally have to negotiate with several government departments to achieve your goal. For example, when the St. Lawrence Cement Company decided to build a new $300 million coal-fired cement plant in the Hudson Valley south of Albany in 1999, it faced the daunting challenge of securing seventeen permits from various local, state, and federal departments and agencies before it could turn over one shovel of ground. That meant it had to engage in at least seventeen separate negotiations, a process that would go on for years.[1]

In many other situations, you negotiate with a government not to obtain a benefit, but to avoid or reduce a burden. At the end of an IRS audit, you may negotiate hard to escape a tax penalty. When you are stopped by a state trooper for speeding on the highway, you may try to negotiate to avoid a ticket. And if you get in real trouble with the law, you will likely find yourself engaged in plea bargaining with the prosecutor since that is the way the vast majority of criminal prosecutions end.

While we may like to think that we live in a world dominated by private enterprise, where the state is increasingly ceding its economic role to private persons and companies, governments, both in the United States and abroad, are still powerful players with whom all businesses and organizations must learn to deal. Governments regulate and tax business activity. They buy from and sell to private companies. They invest as partners in all manner of deals. So being in business means you have to learn to deal with governments. Organizations in the non-profit world, like charities, universities, and museums, also deal regularly with governments, whether they are seeking government grants, service contracts, or just permission to operate. Indeed, if you are the leader of a *state* college, *municipal* hospital, or a *federal* institute, you are engaged in a constant process of negotiating with both the legislative and executive branches of some government in order to obtain the budget you need to function and at the same time preserve your autonomy from government control.

Few organizations today have the luxury or even the possibility of functioning without negotiating with some government unit in some way. As a result, most substantial companies and organizations have established and staffed sizable "government affairs" or "government relations" departments and offices whose primary function is to deal with—that is, *to negotiate with*—governments. In this connection, they also often have outposts in Washington, D.C., Albany, N.Y., or Brussels, Belgium, in order to be close to the governmental authorities they negotiate with.

Hired Help for Individuals and Organizations Dealing with Governments

Regardless of what the law may say, it's not easy for an individual or a private organization to actually engage a government in meaningful negotiations. Governments are usually busy, big, and powerful. Despite their size, they often suffer from a shortage of staff and resources necessary to accomplish the tasks they are supposed to carry out. Consequently, the many persons and organizations that seek their attention often find that dealing with a government is a lengthy and in some cases futile process. Moreover, for the ordinary citizen with a problem or an issue needing government attention, it is often difficult to know which governmental officials can handle the problem, where they are located, how to contact them and secure a hearing, and if a meeting is granted how to persuade them to take action in the citizen's favor. So even though the U.S. Constitution guarantees you the "right to petition," you may not have the knowledge, experience, contacts, and resources to engage in meaningful and effective petitioning that will allow you to advance your interests.

In order to overcome the special challenges of negotiating with governments, many organizations hire third persons, such as lobbyists, advisors, and lawyers, with the necessary expertise, relationships, and access to help in government negotiations. Third parties with special access to and knowledge of government have probably existed to help in negotiating with governments since the very idea of government began. Throughout history, courtiers, scribes, hangers-on, royal relatives, and aristocratic mistresses were always available for a fee or a favor to help bring a citizen's petition to the attention of the king.

Today, individuals and organizations spend billions of dollars each year employing lobbyists, law firms, and public relations organizations to help them with this ages-old task. As a result, these third parties have become permanent fixtures in any significant negotiations with government, and few companies would consider undertaking governmental negotiations without this kind of hired help.

In 2003, when the U.S. president and the Congress began to

consider the addition of a prescription drug benefit to the federal Medicare program, the pharmaceutical and health care industries, along with their trade associations, launched a massive lobbying campaign involving some 950 lobbyists (30 of whom were former senators or members of Congress) and the expenditure of $141 million to shape the policies governing this new benefit to their advantage. Ironically, one of the rules that the pharmaceutical industry succeeded in writing into legislation was a provision that *prohibits* the Federal Government's Center for Medicare Services from negotiating with drug companies to secure discounted prices on the purchase of drugs by Medicare subscribers, thereby preventing the Center from using its potentially enormous bargaining power on their behalf. Here then was a unique case of private parties negotiating hard to prevent the government from negotiating with them in the future.[2]

The Public as Participant

Unlike most negotiations between private parties, negotiations with governments often take on a public dimension. Because the public interest is always potentially present any time that an individual deals with a government, any interaction that begins as a *bilateral* negotiation between you and a governmental unit has the potential to evolve quickly into a *multilateral* negotiation involving persons who at first did not seem directly involved in your transaction but have now suddenly become passionate participants. For example, a motorcycle enthusiast who began a negotiation with the town planning board to obtain a permit to build a racing track on his residential land soon found himself engaged in heated negotiations with his neighbors who objected to it. And the St. Lawrence Cement Company began negotiations with various government departments to build its new plant but within a short time was embroiled in negotiations with half the upper Hudson Valley who opposed its plans.

The potential intervention of members of the public is thus another important difference between purely private negotiations and negotiations with governments. As a result, you need to plan for this possibility and involve your public relations experts in your negotiating team from the start to deal with this possibility. Large projects, necessitating government approvals, like the construction of a factory or a shopping mall, inevitably provoke public concern that will powerfully influence a negotiation that you thought concerned only you and the government official on the other side of the table. So in any negotiation with a government, be ready for the intervention of the public, invited or not. That intervention can often have a negative effect on your negotiations with government departments and even prevent you from attaining your goals, as both the motorcycle enthusiast and the St. Lawrence Cement Company painfully learned.

The Purposes of Negotiating with Governments

Individuals and organizations engage in dealing with governments for one of two purposes:

1. To secure agreement on a transaction.
2. To obtain a rule that favors their interests.

Let's take a look at each of these objectives.

Negotiating Transactions

The purpose of most of our dealings with governments is to achieve a desired transaction in which government is a participant, such as a contract to sell software to the Defense Department, or for which government approval is necessary, such as authorization to open a new charter school. Your avoidance of an IRS tax penalty or a speeding ticket is also a transaction that results from your negotiation with an agent of a government. As we will see, such transactions with governments and the very process by which they are made are almost always subject to complex rules found in laws and regulations applicable to the governmental unit on the other side of the negotiating table.

Negotiating Rules

Private parties not only negotiate transactions with governments, they also negotiate with governments about the very content of the rules themselves. The rules to which we are subject in laws and regulations are not only the product of the give and take of the legislative and regulatory processes, they are very much a result of negotiations between private persons and organizations on the one hand and individual legislators and regulators on the other. Private individuals, small businesses, large corporations, non-profit organizations, and indeed other government agencies are in a constant process of communicating with members of the House and Senate, state legislators, governors, and even the president of the United States in order to shape rules in ways that will favor their interests. Indeed, these kinds of communications are considered a fundamental part of the democratic process and are protected by the U.S. Constitution as the exercise of the "right of petition," a right guaranteed by the First Amendment, which provides that "Congress shall make no law . . . abridging . . . the right of the people . . . to petition the Government for a redress of grievances." So citizens have a right to try to persuade various branches of government to make new rules or to change old ones. They exercise that right in many ways. They write letters to their state representatives, they buttonhole their congressional representatives at political dinners, they visit their senators' offices in Washington, D.C., and they hire lobbyists to present their proposals to the "right person" in the "right government office."

On the other hand, although citizens have a right to communicate with government, the government under the Constitution has no obligation to respond or even pay attention to those petitions. As the Supreme Court has explained, "nothing in the First Amendment or in this Court's case law interpreting it suggests that the rights to speak, associate, and petition require government policymakers to listen or respond to individuals' communications on public issues."[3] In short, as a matter of U.S. constitutional law and indeed the laws of most other countries, the government doesn't have to negotiate with you if it doesn't want to.

Nonetheless, basic electoral politics in democratic countries usually make elected officials listen to and try to respond to the specific concerns and requests of private citizens and organizations, if they hope to stay in office for very long. Members of city councils, state representatives, and U.S. senators spend a large part of each day listening to and responding to the concerns of their constituents. And despite the Supreme Court's view of the right of petition, many specific laws may require particular government agencies and officials to respond to and deal with citizen complaints, requests, and suggestions. For example, when an agency is proposing to make a new rule, such as an effort by the U.S. Securities and Exchange Commission (SEC) to change the requirements for mutual fund governance, it will ordinarily set in motion a process of announcing its proposal and requesting comments from the public. While government and elected officials may avoid calling these kinds of communications between citizens and the government "negotiations," they nonetheless often demonstrate the back-and-forth quality of interactions between persons that characterizes a negotiation.

Negotiated Rulemaking

Recognizing the inherent, though often unstated negotiating quality of much rulemaking, the U.S. government and certain states have instituted and employed a special procedure for the last quarter century called "negotiated rulemaking." Through this process, a government agency seeking to make rules to govern a particularly contentious area, such as the environment or worker health and safety, will convene the representatives of the various affected interest groups who, with the aid of a facilitator, will try to negotiate a recommendation on the proposed rule to the agency. This agency will then use the recommendation as the basis for the rule or regulation it will issue. Negotiated rulemaking, sometimes referred to as "reg-neg" (regulatory negotiation) has been employed in a wide variety of areas, including the Department of Transportation regulations on delivering propane and other compressed gases, the Occupational Safety and Health Administration

(OSHA) rules concerning the erection of steel structures, and the State of California rules on air quality.

Negotiated rulemaking procedure, itself governed by a specific set of rules, is a formal and explicit recognition that negotiation among private persons, companies, and government agencies is an appropriate process for making rules and regulations. For its proponents, the advantages of this process are that it reduces the adversarial nature of rule making, allows for more creative solutions, and achieves better outcomes for all concerned because all relevant interests are represented. Moreover, negotiated rules are less likely to be challenged in the courts because of the greater likelihood that they have taken account of the diverse concerns of those to whom the rules will be applied.[4]

The Processes for Negotiating with Governments

Many people who have to deal with government do not view their activities as negotiations and do not consider themselves negotiators in those settings. Rather, persons and organizations dealing with governments, either to secure a transaction or to obtain a favorable rule, tend to see themselves as supplicants, not much different from the traditional image of the peasant who stands hat in hand before the king or the lord of the manor to humbly beg a favor.

On the other side, government officials involved in dealing with private parties view themselves as merely carrying out the laws and regulations they are obligated to apply. They are *dispensers* of the transactions that the law allows, not negotiators. As one official from the Mexican Central Bank told me, "For government officials, negotiation is not proper. Law is not a negotiable thing when you are in charge of applying it." So, an initial problem is how to characterize interactions between private parties and government agencies when a private party is trying to advance its interests. Can one say that seeking a permit, license, permission, subsidy, or new rule from a government agency or office is a "negotiation?" Similarly, when you are pleading with a state trooper not to give you a ticket or with an IRS agent not to impose a tax penalty, are you "negotiating?"

Negotiation Defined

Negotiations do not require a polished bargaining table, a team of lawyers, or reams of detailed documents. Negotiation is basically *a process of communication by which two or more parties seek to advance their own interests or those of the persons they represent through an agreement on a desired future action.* The parties to a negotiation are involved in that communication because at least one side has decided that it can improve its situation in some way if both sides agree on some act that requires the participation of both sides, such as the sale of a house, the formation of a partnership, or the licensing of a trademark. That communication process can happen through a variety of means, including a meeting between executives in a conference room, a casual one-on-one conversation at a cocktail party, a telephone call in the middle of the night, or an exchange of e-mails with a company on the other side of the world. By this definition, your tense conversations with an IRS agent at the end of an audit and with a state trooper at the side of a highway are most definitely negotiations.

Similarly, the process of obtaining a building permit from the town, a school charter from the state, or a contract from the Defense Department is also a negotiation. You are engaging in communications with the concerned government department or agency in hopes of advancing your interests by persuading that government department or agency to agree to grant you the permit, charter, or contract you need. On the other side of the communication, the government agency is engaged in the communication because it believes that it also has a chance to advance its own interests or the interests of the public it is supposed to represent. But unlike most private parties involved in negotiations, the government agency concerned is usually engaged in the communication process because some law or regulation authorizes or even requires it to deal with private parties on this matter. Thus the state education law requires the Department of Education to consider requests for school charters and the local zoning law obligates the town planning board to review and decide on building permits. Moreover, that same law will usually specify in some detail how that agency is to conduct such interactions—such negotiations—with private citizens.

Discretion Is the Opening to Negotiation

The fact that a law or regulation requires or authorizes a government department to engage in a communication with a private party in order to grant that private party a benefit or privilege does not deprive that interaction of the quality of being a "negotiation." Despite the Mexican official's protestations, few systems established by law make automatic, mechanical decisions. Because lawmakers do not have perfect foresight, no law or regulation that they make can provide for all possible eventualities that may happen in the future. If lawmakers did attempt to legislate to cover all future possibilities, it is likely that they would create a system that would be rigid, cumbersome, slow, and unable to adapt to changing circumstances. As a result, all governmental systems require in varying degrees that their operators exercise some degree of *discretion* in making their decisions, whether it is granting a school charter, issuing a building permit, or purchasing software. Discretion in this context means the ability to make a decision involving a choice among various options.

Law and regulations are made with words—words whose application requires interpretation. Much negotiation with government officials involves the interpretation of words found in laws, regulations, and policies, as the private party involved seeks to persuade a government official to interpret those words in ways that will favor the private party's interests. For example, a local zoning ordinance may provide that only "one-family residences and customary accessory uses of a one-family residence" may be built in a designated area of a town. Certainly a sandbox for the children and a swimming pool for the family would be considered a customary accessory use of a residence. But what about a thirty-foot-wide motorcycle track for a homeowner who is a motorcycle enthusiast? The Zoning Board of Appeals in the village of Taghkanic, New York, faced that precise issue in 2006 when the homeowner, a New Jersey banker, wanted to pursue his passion at one of his country homes. After lengthy discussions involving the homeowner, neighbors, and other members of the public, the zoning board decided that a motorcycle race course was not a "customary accessory use" by a divided vote of 3 to 1.[5]

Whenever a governmental department has the discretion to decide or not decide in your favor, you are involved in negotiations, whether you recognize it or not. Like the motorcycle enthusiast in upstate New York, your challenge in dealing with a government in those situations is to persuade an official, department, or agency to exercise its discretion in your favor—to grant the building permit, to deliver the school charter, to purchase the software.

In negotiating with any government official, one of your first challenges is to determine precisely how much discretion that person has. As a general rule, government regulators are often reluctant to say how much discretion they have in an individual case. One often hears a government official say "my hands are tied" in answer to a request for action that is out of the ordinary. In order to determine the scope of that person's discretion, you not only have to examine the laws and regulations under which they operate but also what they have done in the past. As we shall see in Chapter 6, past actions by that official, the official's department, or similar governmental units are powerful indicators of the real discretion that a government official actually has. On the other hand, in your interactions with that official, you never want to take the position that he or she can apply or ignore any legal provisions they wish, because that attitude may convey the idea that you think the official is not bound by or following the law.

In reality of course, few laws or regulations are so specific that their application is completely automatic. Every government official has some degree of discretion in interpreting and applying the laws and regulations he or she is supposed to implement. The Food and Drug Administration can decide or not decide to approve the sale of a new drug that a pharmaceutical company has spent the last ten years developing and testing. The European Union Competition Directorate General has discretion to approve or prohibit the acquisition by a U.S. multinational of a European computer manufacturer. Your local zoning board has discretion to allow you to put an addition on your house and perhaps even to build a motorcycle race track in your backyard. This does not mean, of course, that these governmental units can make any decision they wish. They are accountable for the exercise of their discretion to the public and to the courts in a variety of ways. They have to exercise that discretion in accordance with certain accepted rules and principles. Nonetheless, those rules and principles give them varying degrees of discretion. And the exercise of that discretion is a subject of negotiation. You therefore need to understand both the precise limits of the discretion that the official or agency may have and the rules and principles that govern the exercise of that discretion.

The Substance and Procedure of Discretion

Even if the law or regulation is clear on the *substance* of the transaction you are negotiating, the government official may nonetheless have wide discretion on *the process or procedure to* be followed in making the governmental decision that is the subject of your negotiation. For example, the official may have discretion to act quickly on your request or to let it languish for months on the bottom of the pile of papers on her desk. She may assign an experienced and highly competent person to negotiate with you on the transaction, or an inexperienced novice who hasn't a clue. She may have discretion to provide you with valuable background information and guidance or let you educate yourself on government processes as best you can. This discretion over procedure and how that official uses it can have a direct impact on your ability to get what you want from a government department. You therefore need to focus on both procedure and substance in your negotiation with any government department.

The Dangers of Discretion

Although governmental discretion is necessary to make the system run, *unchecked* exercise of discretion by governmental officials can also result in abuse and corruption. While corruption has many legal definitions, it is basically the abuse of a public office for private gain. Corruption arises in negotiations with governments when government negotiators employ their discretion to advance their own personal interests, instead of the interests of the government and the public they are supposed to represent.

Although most public officials throughout the world work diligently for their governments, corruption is a particular risk in negotiation with governments. It can take many forms: cash payments to an official to secure a government contract, gifts to a politician's spouse to gain that politician's endorsement of a permit, or an interest-free "loan" to the brother of a tax official reviewing your company's tax returns during the last five years.

In 2004, Darleen Druyan, the second ranking procurement officer for the U.S. Air Force and a long-time member of the Defense Department bureaucracy, who controlled an acquisition budget of $30 billion a year, went to prison when it was discovered that she had consistently favored Boeing in her negotiations on aircraft purchases in order to secure jobs at Boeing for her daughter and her son-in-law, as well as a position for herself as the company's Deputy General Manager of Missile Defense Systems at a salary of $250,000 a year, plus a $50,000 signing bonus.[6] As this case indicates, governmental corruption is by no means limited to poor third-world countries. In fact in 2006, Transparency International, a non-profit organization that tracks governmental corruption around the world, found that the United States was tied with Chile and Belgium for twentieth in its Corruption Perceptions Index, meaning that seventeen other countries, including Switzerland, Denmark, and Singapore, were perceived as less corrupt than the United States.[7]

The existence of a corrupt official on the other side of the negotiating table can obstruct your negotiation in two ways. First, it may confront you with the choice of walking away from the deal or engaging in an illegal act by paying a bribe. Second, if you are in competition for a deal with another company that has made a corrupt payment, you may lose the deal for reasons that you do not fathom. That was precisely the situation of Boeing's competitors who could not understand how Boeing had beaten them in the competition to sell aircraft to the U.S. Defense Department.

Corruption, as Robert Klitgaard has pointed out, is a function of three factors: discretion, monopoly, and accountability.[8] The likelihood of corruption by government official arises when the official has great discretion, when that official has monopoly power over the other person in the negotiation, and when mechanisms for holding the official accountable for his or her actions are weak. Darleen Druyan had almost unfettered discretion in setting prices for aircraft purchases, she held monopoly power since airplane manufacturers had to deal with her and her alone to sell their products to the Air Force, and there were few mechanisms to review her actions or hold her accountable for the exercise of her decision. Although she held the second ranking procurement position, the heads of Air Force procurement had always been political appointees who served for short periods of time and never were able to achieve the power and influence that she possessed within the Defense Department bureaucracy in her long career. She effectively had unfettered control over aircraft purchases for the U.S. Air Force.

The potential for corruption in negotiating with government is always present and you should be alert to its presence. We offer a few suggestions for dealing with corruption in your negotiations with government in Chapter 3.

Negotiation by Any Other Name

Despite the widespread prevalence of negotiations between government departments and private citizens and organizations, many government officials, like the one from the Mexican Central Bank, strongly resist the idea that when they do their jobs they are engaged in "negotiation." An understanding of the reason for this attitude provides some useful insights into government officials as negotiators and indeed into the whole process of negotiating with governments.

First, many officials take comfort in the fiction that their decisions are made according to rules, automatically applied. Thus, in a sense their decisions are not their responsibility, but that of the legislature that made the rules applied by the official. If you as a citizen don't like that decision, you should blame the legislature that made the rule, not the public official who merely applied it. This fiction is a means of protecting the official against complaints and criticism from various interest groups and individuals. For an official to acknowledge that the issuance of a permit resulted from a negotiation, which implies a back-and-forth exchange of proposals and counterproposals, is to admit that the decision did not result from an automatic application of the rules. Such admissions would open officials to questions, challenges, and threats that might undermine their positions and injure their careers.

Second, for many people, compromise is implicit in the notion of negotiation. Although the public accepts compromise in certain contexts, it considers compromise inappropriate in others. For example, while it is one thing for a business executive to acknowledge engaging in compromise when negotiating a merger with another private company, it is quite another thing for a public official to admit compromise in granting a permit. In the public's view, the application of public policy, law, and regulations is not to be subjected to compromise. Rather, the public expects governments to apply law, regulations, and policies uniformly to all persons. To accept the notion that the application of laws and regulations is the product of negotiation and that therefore some persons benefit from them and others don't is in many ways an affront to our basic notions of democracy and equality before the law. For most officials and regulators, a model government decision with respect to a company or individual is objective, impersonal, and uniform. A negotiated decision, on the other hand, implies just the opposite. A negotiated decision is subjective, personal, and special to the party concerned. What this means is that in many of your interactions with governments, it is often best to avoid the word "negotiation" in referring to the process in which you are engaged. To respect governmental sensitivities, call your negotiations with government officials by any other name: discussions, conversations, requests, or interactions.

Conclusion: Seven Power Tools and Seven Secrets for Negotiating with Governments

Despite public perceptions and bureaucratic fictions, government decisions affecting individuals and organizations are by and large the product of negotiation. The basic problem for most of us in our negotiations with governments, whether local, state, national, or foreign, is that all the power in those interactions seems to sit on the other side of the table from us. The purpose of this book is to help you negotiate more effectively with governments by changing that balance of power. To do that, it offers you seven power tools to increase your ability to influence government decisions in your favor. Just as power tools increase the productivity and effectiveness of carpenters and mechanics, these negotiation power tools will lead to better results in your negotiations with governments. The seven power tools on which this book is based are the following:

Power Tool #1. Counterpart Evaluation. "Governments feel different," an experienced corporate dealmaker once told me. What he meant was that governments as negotiators are not like private parties. They approach, prepare for, conduct, and conclude negotiations in ways that are different from how individuals and corporations do. In order to deal with governments effectively, private persons and companies must understand these differences and develop strategies to cope with them. Chapter 2 explores those differences, focusing particularly on the inherent strengths and weaknesses of government officials as negotiators.

Power Tool #2. Preparation. Successful negotiation requires effective preparation. Chapter 3 discusses the way to get ready for government negotiations, both with respect to preparing yourself and preparing the ground. Effective preparation increases your power in any negotiation.

Power Tool #3. Organizational Analysis. All governments are embedded in an organizational structure. Understanding and penetrating that structure is an important first step in trying to negotiate with it. Chapter 4 considers the role of government structure in negotiations and how to understand the best ways to overcome organizational obstacles.

Power Tool #4. Interests. All negotiations are driven by the interests of the negotiators. Governments as negotiators have special interests—interests that are influenced by what one may call "the political imperative." Chapter 5 explains the nature of those interests and how they affect your negotiation.

Power Tool #5. Influence Techniques. The goal of any negotiator is to influence the other side in desired ways. Chapter 6 presents various techniques you can employ to influence government decisions in your negotiations.

Power Tool #6. Third Parties. As indicated earlier, a whole range of organizations and individuals exist to help with governmental negotiations. Chapter 7 explores the role of third persons in government negotiations, particularly lobbyists, experts, and agents, how to use them best, and how to avoid or at least minimize their risks and costs.

Power Tool #7. Renegotiation. One of the risks of government negotiations is that governments tend to see any deal they make as always being open to reconsideration and renegotiation, even after the contract has been signed, when it suits that government's interests. Former Secretary of State George Shultz, an experienced government hand, captured the essence of this phenomenon when he said, "It's never over."[9] More than a century earlier, British Prime Minister Benjamin Disraeli expressed the same idea more elegantly when he told the House of Commons: "Finality is not the language of politics." Chapter 8 explains how to cope with the constant risk of governmental renegotiation of deals that you thought were signed, sealed, and delivered.

The seven power tools outlined above challenge at least seven important tenets of conventional wisdom about dealings between private parties and governments, or at least the conventional wisdom governments themselves usually assert. To that extent, these tools are based on seven secrets for negotiating with governments—and coming out ahead.

Secret #1: Governments ~~don't~~ *DO* negotiate with private parties about anything.

Secret #2: Governments are *NOT* all-powerful in their dealing with private parties.

Secret #3: Governments are *NOT* united monoliths in those dealings.

Secret #4: Governments *DO NOT* seek only to advance the public interest in their negotiations.

Secret #5: Governments ~~aren't~~ *ARE* susceptible to influence techniques by private parties.

Secret #6: Governments ~~don't~~ *DO* accept third-party interventions in their negotiation with individuals.

Secret #7: Government decisions, once made, ~~aren't~~ *ARE* open to renegotiation.

In the following chapters, we will explain how to apply these secrets and use these tools in your negotiations with local, state, national, or foreign governments.

• CHAPTER TWO •

Governments Feel Different

How Negotiating with a Government Differs from Negotiating with Anyone Else

> "The government's view of the economy can be summed up in a few short phrases: If it moves, tax it. If it keeps moving, regulate it. If it stops moving, subsidize it."
>
> —U.S. PRESIDENT RONALD REAGAN[1]

If governments as negotiating counterparts feel different from private organizations, it is because of two factors: the special *powers of* governments and the special *constraints on* governments.

Governments have special powers that private persons and companies don't have. Microsoft is one of the wealthiest and most technologically advanced companies in the world, but it still doesn't have the powers that a poor third-world government like Bangladesh can exercise both within and outside of its borders. For all its resources, Microsoft cannot seize property, use force to secure its will, conduct diplomatic relations with countries, and be a member of international organizations. Bangladesh can and does do all of these things.

At the same time, despite their powers, governments labor under special political constraints that no private company no matter how large or small must deal with. For example, while a family-run grocery store in Des Moines, Iowa, is dwarfed by the power and wealth of the U.S. government, that same grocery store is also free in negotiating with its suppliers of the numerous political and legal constraints that the government departments must cope with in negotiating with their own suppliers.

The nature and extent of government powers and constraints will of course vary from government to government and from country to country. But in preparing to negotiate with any government you should seek to understand the special powers of that government, as well as the special constraints that affect its ability to use those powers. That knowledge will help you devise the negotiating strategies and tactics to attain your goals in the negotiation.

Four Powers and Four Constraints

All governments tend to apply four types of powers and at the same time labor under four political constraints in their negotiations with private persons and companies. In addition to their natural attributes derived from their wealth and resources, all governments derive special powers from:

1. Their monopoly position
2. Their special governmental privileges and immunities
3. Their role as defenders of the public interest and welfare
4. Their special protocols and forms

At the same time, their negotiations are constrained by:

1. The rules that they must follow in negotiations
2. Pressures from their constituents
3. Bureaucratic incentives and interests of their organizations
4. Their operational norms

Let's look first at the special powers that governments bring to negotiations.

Governments' Special Powers

Governments readily apply their special powers in negotiations with individuals. You need to understand their strengths and limitations in order to cope with them when you negotiate.

Power #1: The Power of Monopoly

Most of the time, when you are negotiating with other individuals and companies, you have alternative courses of action if the negotiations fail. If you are trying to make a deal with a particular distributor to handle your products, you know that you have the option of seeking other possible distributors if you can't reach agreement. If you are negotiating to acquire another company as part of your strategy of corporate growth, you usually have yet another company as a possible target for acquisition. These alternatives may be good or bad, but other options do exist.

The nature and extent of your other options affect your bargaining power in a negotiation. To the extent that you have other good options, you have a position of strength in negotiation. To the extent that your alternatives are poor, you have less power. So if there is strong market demand for your product or service, you have many options and will therefore be able to play a strong hand at the negotiating table. If market demand is weak, your negotiating power will be proportionately reduced.

Most of the time when we negotiate with governments, we are negotiating with an entity that has a monopoly over what we are seeking. As a result, we know that we have few other options, if any, to satisfy our interests. That realization has the effect of giving us a sense that we are in a weak bargaining position when we negotiate with a government department. In short, we perceive that in negotiating with a government, our alternatives for making a deal are usually not very good. For instance, if you want to sell a drug in the United States, you have to obtain approval from the Food and Drug Administration (FDA), and the Food and Drug Administration alone. You can't go to the SEC, the IRS, or OSHA to get one. The FDA's monopoly position gives it a position of power in its negotiations with pharmaceutical companies. Similarly, if you want to build an extension to your home to accommodate your growing family, you have many choices in selecting a building contractor, but you have only one choice for obtaining the required building permit: your local planning board. If pharmaceutical companies had several possible agencies from which to obtain a drug approval, their negotiating position would clearly be enhanced. If you had a choice of departments from which to obtain a building permit, you would feel a lot more confident about putting that new extension on your house.

Sometimes you may have to negotiate with another company that has a dominant position in the market, like a Microsoft or a Wal-Mart, a position that seems close to a monopoly. The difference between negotiating with a Microsoft or a Wal-Mart on the one hand and a government on the other is that a government usually has a *legal* monopoly over what you are seeking. That legal monopoly makes it impervious to various market factors, such as share price or technological change, that strongly influence a Wal-Mart or Microsoft, no matter how dominant it is for the time being.

Governments' legal monopoly makes them impervious to market forces and gives them a sense of permanence that few companies in the private sector enjoy. Also, unlike a company that has a dominant market position, a government department has the ability to use force to protect its legal monopoly. So if you try to sell that drug without FDA approval, federal authorities will close down your plant and probably put you in jail. If you build that extension without the building permit from the town, the town can force you to tear it down and fine you for violating the building code.

The monopoly position of governmental units, coupled with their ability to use force to assert it, is one important factor that gives negotiations with government a different nature and dynamic from negotiations between two private parties. It is this factor that makes us feel that we are in a weak bargaining position when we sit across the table from a government negotiator. It is this factor that makes us feel like supplicants, rather than negotiators, in our dealing with governments. It is also this factor that tends to color the whole interaction between the government and the private party throughout the course of the negotiation. One can readily understand then why pharmaceutical companies, having to deal with the monopoly power of government to secure approvals to sell drugs to the public, did not want to face that same government monopoly power in actually selling drugs to Medicare subscribers. They therefore used their own considerable influence with Congress to secure legislation that prevents federal Medicare officials from negotiating lower drug prices on subscribers' behalf.

A government's monopoly position is also strengthened by that fact that its financial ability to function is not usually dependent in any way on its success in negotiations. Negotiations between two private companies usually have some impact on both sides' finances and that factor influences their actions in the negotiations. For example, in a negotiation between a manufacturer and a distributor, the prospect of financial gain or loss influences the kind of deals they make and the way they make them. A series of failed negotiations may mean reduced profits and therefore declining fortunes for a private company. That prospect often makes private parties more ready to compromise at the bargaining table.

Most government departments, on the other hand, operate on the basis of annual legislative appropriations of tax revenues. Their budgets are unaffected by the success or failure of the negotiations that their departments undertake. For example, while the success or failure of a real estate developer to secure a building permit from the city building department for a shopping mall will have major consequences for its revenues and profits, the results of the negotiation will have no effect whatsoever on the operating revenues of the city building department. This factor, when combined with government's monopoly to decide on the subject of the negotiation, gives government departments a powerful bargaining position in any negotiation. It means that their alternatives to not making an agreement (unlike yours) are by no means terribly bad. If you fail in your negotiations with the government, you may go out of business tomorrow. The government department on the other hand is assured of continuing to operate tomorrow pretty much as it did yesterday no matter whether its negotiation with you succeeds or fails.

The fact that in most cases when we negotiate with a government we are negotiating with a *monopoly* provider makes our success in the negotiation seem crucial and failure extremely costly. A pharmaceutical company's inability to gain FDA approval for a new drug means that it will be closed out of the biggest pharmaceutical market in the world. The failure to get a permit to put an addition on your home will probably mean that you either have to put two kids in one bedroom or sell the place to buy something bigger.

Governments Can Hurt You Badly

Government negotiators clearly understand the power that their monopoly position gives them in their negotiations, and they are rarely reluctant to use it in pursuing their negotiating objectives. For example, they will implicitly or explicitly threaten to deny what you are seeking to persuade you to take some action or to make some concession that you would prefer not to. So, if a pharmaceutical company wants that drug approval, it will have to accede to FDA demands for another year of testing. If you want that building permit, you will have to scale back the size of that new family room you were planning. Governments' monopoly position in negotiations explains why one experienced government relations specialist concluded our interview with a sigh: "Remember," she said, "governments can hurt you badly." In most negotiations, they hurt you badly not by taking some punitive, affirmative act, but rather by exercising their monopoly power to refuse what you are seeking—to say no. No drug approval. No building permit. No motorcycle race track.

Power #2: The Power of Privilege and Immunity

Governments also feel different from other negotiators because they enjoy many legal privileges and immunities that private companies and persons do not. Not only do they have the power to regulate how businesses operate, they also have the ability to seize property, cancel contracts, threaten force and, if need be, actually use it against you to obtain their objectives. Moreover, in many countries, you can't sue the government in a court of law no matter how arbitrary their actions, nor can you force it to respect the contracts they have signed, no matter how detailed. National legal systems give governments an array of privileges and immunities in order to allow them to perform their basic task of governing.

These extensive privileges and immunities also give governments special authority at the negotiating table. The implicit or explicit threat by a government to exercise its special powers against a counterpart has influenced the results of many negotiations between government units and private corporations. Multinational corporations, while having a vast pool of capital and technology at their command, don't have these kinds of powers. The result, as one senior executive at a giant global pharmaceutical company once told me, is that even "the smallest governments can jerk you around."

Many times, a government's explicit or implicit threat to use this power causes private negotiators to make concessions that they would not normally make in a negotiation with another private company. It is the exercise of this power that often forces companies with advantageous government contracts to renegotiate them and thereby give the government more favorable terms.

One way to reduce this power differential is for a private party to enlist the assistance of another government or organization as an equalizer. So if you are having a problem with a local government in the United States, you might try to get state authorities to help. If you are stymied by a foreign government, you seek help from your own government. Thus U.S. foreign investors whose economic interests are threatened by foreign host country action or inaction often ask the local U.S. embassy to assist in negotiating a solution.

Power #3: The Power of Representing the Public Interest

Governments cloak all of their actions, legal or not, on grounds that they are acting in the public interest rather than for private gain. They normally justify their actions as being for "national security," "public welfare," or "the good of the people." In many negotiations, government officials often take the moral high ground in order to justify their demands and obtain concessions from the other side. They, after all, are altruistically seeking to achieve the public good in the negotiation, while you, as a private company, are merely looking to make a selfish profit. Thus in one negotiation with an African tax official in which I was asserting that the country's "development tax" did not apply to the organization I represented, the official responded with a pained look: "Don't you want to help us develop our country?" He ultimately agreed to grant the exemption, but not before he had made me feel as if I were selfishly putting in jeopardy his country's future through my self-seeking and unreasonable demands.

Away from the bargaining table, the government's role as representative of the public interest also gives it the ability to mobilize popular support for its negotiating positions and to use political influence to gain advantages that no private corporation ever could. For example, during its financial crisis in 2001, the Argentine government refused to pay its international debts, declaring that to do so would threaten the basic welfare of the Argentine people. It portrayed foreign creditors and investors as imperiling the very survival of the country, a tactic that gained the government great popular support and foreign financiers widespread hostility. African governments have used a similar tactic in their negotiations with international pharmaceutical companies to obtain low prices on HIV drugs and other medicines essential to public health.

As a result of this power of governments to represent the public interest, companies engaged in negotiations with governments often find that they must conduct two related but separate negotiations to achieve their objectives: one inside the negotiating room with government representatives and the other outside in the media and in public relations. Indeed, you should keep in mind that almost any negotiation with a government, whether it concerns loans to Argentina or the construction of a motorcycle race track in Taghkanic, New York, has the potential to become a public issue in which civic organizations, nongovernmental organizations, and the public in general take an active, vocal part. As a result, you should plan for this eventuality in shaping your negotiating strategy with any government.

Power #4: The Power of Protocol and Form

Governments and their representatives are usually acutely sensitive to matters concerning their status, prestige, and dignity, since these elements are essential to carrying out their primary task: governing. All other things being equal, a government that is held in high esteem by its people and by other nations will find it easier to govern than a government that does not have the respect of its citizens or of other countries.

One of the ways in which governments seek to preserve and enhance their status and power is through their use of various forms and protocols, particularly those that relate to how private citizens are to communicate and interact with the government and its officials. Governments usually have express or implicit rules about how private persons are to approach them, what form of address they are to use, and where they are to sit or stand in relation to government representatives. Governments consider the failure to respect these forms as a sign of disrespect or, worse, a challenge to their authority.

Governments use these forms in order to enhance their power in a negotiation and they strongly influence governmental actors in their negotiations. For example, when Jane Alexander, an award-winning actress, was appointed by President Clinton as Chairman of the National Endowment for the Arts (NEA), she noted that at her Senate confirmation hearing all the senators sat on a platform some six feet higher than where she sat. Although she had a long career on the stage, she was cowed by this protocol. Later she would reflect, "I don't know when those in power elevated themselves above everyone else, but psychologically it does the trick, reducing the supplicant to a state of intimidation."[2] Alexander's confirmation as head of the NEA, an agency that at that time was the subject of much contention in Congress, was a form of a negotiation with government. In your own negotiations with governments, you should be prepared for their representatives to use protocol and procedures as power tools—means to influence and if need be intimidate you.

As a result of these forms and protocols, government officials frequently bring to the negotiating table attitudes and approaches that seem to introduce rigidity into the deal-making process. By virtue of their governmental status, negotiators for government departments, ministries, and state corporations often behave differently in negotiations than private companies would. For one thing, they resist being considered as equals to the private businesspeople on the other side of the table. Indeed, any suggestion that the two sides are equals may be considered an insult. Government officials represent the "the state," "the nation," and "the people," and a sovereign country, no matter how small, is not the equal of a private business firm, no matter how large. Any slight to a government official may be considered an affront to the dignity of the nation.

In one instance, an African minister asked for a meeting with the head of a foreign mining company that had operations in his country. The meeting took place in the office of the minister of mines and was attended by nine other government ministers. The minister of mines said that the government wanted to renegotiate its concession agreement with the company to obtain a greater share of mineral revenues, and he listed the points that needed to be discussed. In response, the chairman of the mining company reviewed each item, but at one point he flatly said, "We cannot entertain that." To emphasize his position, he struck the table with his hand. The minister immediately adjourned the meeting and refused to continue the discussions.

While the response of the mining company chairman might have been acceptable in a negotiation between two private companies, it was inappropriate in a discussion with what amounted to nearly the entire government of a sovereign state. Instead of an outright rebuff, the chairman should have shown a willingness to listen and to discuss all of the government's concerns. Such flexibility, of course, does not mean that a company has to give in on every point. In this case, it took nearly nine months to get the negotiations going again, and during that time the government made operations difficult for the company. Ultimately, the two sides did renegotiate the mining concession.

Don't Sin Against the Bureaucracy

African government officials are by no means the only ones to look unkindly upon challenges to their authority. You can find similar sensitivities throughout all governments. In 2001, the FDA was dissatisfied with certain aspects of Shering-Plough's manufacturing operations of its asthma inhalers and threatened to withhold approval of the company's new blockbuster allergy medicine Clarinex until the manufacturing problems were solved. A tense meeting between Shering-Plough's top management and FDA officials was held to discuss the matter. When the meeting seemed to have the two sides deadlocked, Shering-Plough's president, Raul Cesan, a hard-driving executive with an assertive style, who had become frustrated with developments in the talks, asked his subordinates to leave the room so that he could talk to the FDA regulators alone. Cesan apparently thought that he could override them with the strength of his personality and strong words. It didn't work. As one of his associates would report later, "Raul is an extremely aggressive guy, but that kind of behavior doesn't go over well with regulators. I don't know what he said, but next week we had inspectors crawling all over every one of our plants."[3]

The lesson of these cases is very clear. In your negotiations with government officials, avoid challenging their authority. As one experienced government affairs professional told me, "You need to give people the respect due their office." A government department's basic capital is its authority. It is authority that enables it to function. If you challenge its authority, either directly or indirectly, you are in effect challenging the ability of that department to perform its basic tasks. When their authority is challenged, the instinct of government officials, like the African ministers and the FDA regulators, is to show you in the clearest possible and most forceful terms that you are wrong. Moreover, having been challenged once by your organization, they will continue to remember that challenge in future dealings for a long time to come. In the theology of government, challenging a government official's authority is a bureaucratic mortal sin. You should bear in mind the wisdom of Admiral Hyman Rickover, the developer of the U.S. nuclear submarine and a redoubtable bureaucratic infighter in his own right: "If you're going to sin, sin against God, not the bureaucracy. God will forgive you, but the bureaucracy won't."[4]

Learn the Necessary Protocols and Forms—and Show Due Respect

Wise negotiators learn the established protocols and forms for dealing with a particular government, and they respect them scrupulously. They also avoid actions that might be considered a challenge to them and thereby to the government itself. Remember, in a negotiation any real or imagined challenge to the authority of a government official—whether a legislator, bureaucrat, or state trooper—is always a bad move, a move that will inevitably prove counterproductive. By virtue of their culture, American negotiators in particular tend to disregard formalities and seek to develop informal relationships with their counterparts on the other side of the table. For example, in a survey that I conducted among 310 negotiators from twelve different cultures, Americans showed the greatest tendency to value and use an informal negotiating style in business dealings.[5] Unfortunately, however, a corporate executive's attempts to be friendly through acts of informality can be interpreted as a lack of respect. General Electric's inability to secure approval of its acquisition of Honeywell from the European Union competition authorities in 2001 is one example. Considering approval a "done deal," GE executives showed little deference to European officials. Early in the discussions, Jack Welch, GE's legendary CEO, said to Mario Monti, EU Competition Commissioner, as if they were in a private business negotiation, "Call me Jack." Monti, keenly aware that he represented the European public interest, replied: "I'll only call you Jack when this deal is over."[6] The talks went downhill from there.

Governments' Special Constraints

A government's monopoly position, its array of privileges and immunities, its role as defender of the public interest, and its forms and protocols give it a clear position of power in its negotiations with private parties. A government in a negotiation with a private company would seem to be in effect an 800-pound gorilla sitting on the other side of the table. On the other hand, few governments are free to use that power in any way they wish. In one way or another, they all are subject to constraints on its use. An understanding of those constraints may allow you to mobilize them to your advantage and thereby reduce the power differential that appears to separate you from the government negotiators on the other side of the table.

Constraint #1: Negotiating Rules

Government bureaucracies exist to apply laws, regulations, and rules. Rules govern all their operations, including their negotiations with private persons and companies. As a result, negotiating with governments is very much a rule-driven process, not the freewheeling interaction that usually characterizes deal-making between purely private parties. Rules and regulations not only affect the kinds of deals governments make but the way they make them.

Rules influence negotiations with governments in two ways: (1) they regulate the negotiation process; and (2) they are often the very subject of the negotiation. First, the negotiation process itself may be subject to rules. For example, if you are trying to sell a product or a service to a government department, you will usually have to follow a set of fairly rigid "procurement rules," normally embodied in detailed laws and regulations that usually have no equivalent in the private sector. So if you want to sell your products or services to the U.S. government, the Federal Acquisition Regulations will control your negotiations. In addition, depending on what you are selling and the department you are dealing with, you will also have to cope with the Armed Services Procurement Act, the Federal Administrative Services Act, and the Competition in Contracting Act, none of which will affect your negotiations with Wal-Mart, Citigroup, or Barclays Bank when you want to sell the same products and services to them.

The rules incorporated in these laws and regulations will tell you how you are to engage the concerned government office, what kind of documentation you must present to it, and the precise terms that will need to appear in your sales contract, and much, much more. Their effect is to limit the freedom of contract of governmental departments, agencies, and state corporations and your own interactions with them. Government officials may be required to use standard form contracts that include mandatory clauses on payment terms, insurance, and guarantees, to mention just a few. They may also be required to favor certain kinds of business over others, for example by giving preference to national companies over foreign companies. Rigid rules and regulations may limit the kind of transactions they may make and the way they can make them.

The Choreography of Government Negotiations

Like an elaborate ballet, the entire process may follow a strict choreography to its completion. Thus, making a deal to sell your products to the government often requires you to engage in distinct, intricate phases—tendering, evaluation, selection, and challenge—each of which is governed by detailed rules. The first phase is *tendering*, whereby the government announces its needs and requests interested and qualified persons to make an offer of the services or goods to be procured. Often, the tendering phases provides for a sealed bidding process. Next, the bids are subjected to evaluation, using criteria that have been decided upon and made public. Once the evaluation is completed, the government agency makes a selection and proceeds to enter into a formal agreement. But before such agreement is finalized, a process of challenge is possible, whereby disappointed bidders are given an opportunity to contest the selection decision. The whole process is time-consuming, costly, and complicated, and often requires the services of persons specialized in this archaic dance.

Few companies in the private sector would conduct negotiations in this fashion, for the simple reason that it would not be "efficient" in the sense of achieving the maximum output for a given input. Here then is a further major difference between negotiations with governments and negotiations between purely private parties. Whereas ostensible "efficiency" is the highest goal sought by private negotiators, ostensible "fairness" is the goal sought by government negotiations. One of the reasons that purely private negotiations value efficiency so highly is that the participants' organizations will directly benefit from any savings or gains achieved in the negotiations. A win-win solution that allows both companies to save money or create new wealth in a particular transaction will have the result that both companies have increased earnings for investment in other projects and for possible distribution to shareholders.

A gain secured for a government in a negotiation, on the other hand, does not benefit the department concerned but passes directly to the state budget, without having a positive impact on the department's own resources. The inability of a government department to capture gains may influence the government negotiator's reluctance to try innovative solutions to problems, particularly if those innovative solutions are not specifically authorized by the rules and might be challenged by third parties as "unfair."

To say that the purpose of such rules and regulations is to assure that negotiations are "fair" does not mean that they are fair to the government or fair to the private party that gets the contract; rather, they must be "fair" to those who did not succeed in making a contract with the government—and to the public as well. In order to protect the government department concerned from accusations of unfairness, arbitrariness, or corruption, the department will defend itself by showing that it has followed the rules in all respects, not by demonstrating that the deal is economically efficient. As a result, the process of conducting a negotiation according to the rules often becomes an end in itself. Because the rules on negotiations have such a central place in negotiations with governments, it is important for private individuals and companies to understand the laws and regulations affecting the governmental department or state-owned corporation whose representatives are sitting on the other side of the table. In the negotiation, the power to convince government officials will almost always depend on your ability to find a rule to justify your position.

Negotiating about Rules

Rules not only govern the negotiation with a government but are often the very subject of that negotiation. The substance of the discussion may also be about rules: about whether one rule or another applies to a transaction or whether a particular regulation can be interpreted to allow or prevent the governmental action that you need. For example, if you are seeking Justice Department approval for a merger or town planning permit to build a shopping center, much of the negotiation will be about how the antitrust rules or the zoning regulations apply or do not apply to the activities that you are proposing to undertake. Often in negotiations with governments, it is less convincing to bureaucrats and therefore less important as strategy to demonstrate that what you are seeking to achieve is good for the public than it is to show that the applicable rules support your case. And when a rule clearly prevents you from meeting your goal, you may undertake negotiation, often through the help of a lobbyist, to change that rule, sometimes with the agency that made it, sometimes with a branch of government that has power over that agency. For example, as U.S. corporations experienced the high costs of complying with the 2002 Sarbanes-Oxley Act, rapidly enacted in the wake of the Enron scandal, they began a process of seeking to change or eliminate some of its more costly provisions.

Rules over Rhetoric

Because of the importance of rules in your negotiations with governments, it is often vital to find a rule that justifies what you are seeking in your negotiation. The fact that no rule prohibits what you are asking may not be enough to convince the officials sitting across the table. If a government department is presented with two possible courses of action, one that is clearly authorized by the prevailing law or regulation and the other only vaguely permitted, that department will almost always favor the first and look dubiously on the second. For example, both the public and the press have criticized the Tennessee Valley Authority (TVA) for focusing its efforts on building dams and generating power, rather than on comprehensive planning for the development of the Tennessee Valley watershed as President Franklin Delano Roosevelt had called for when he introduced legislation to create the TVA in 1933. One of the reasons that the TVA single-mindedly built dams and ignored planning was that its authorizing legislation specifically directed it to build dams but nowhere clearly authorized watershed planning.

Similarly, during the late 1970s, when Egypt began to open up its doors to foreign investment after they had been closed for over twenty years, President Sadat gave glowing speeches about Egypt's openness to and need for foreign investment and warmly urged investors to establish their operations in the country. Drawn by this rhetoric, investors were disappointed to find that the Egyptian bureaucracy was slow to approve their investment proposals. When investors pointed to the speeches that Sadat had been giving as justification for expediting approvals in their negotiations with the Egyptian Investment Authority, Egyptian bureaucrats replied that their job was to apply the law and rules governing investment, not the speeches of President Sadat. The Egyptian laws and regulations on foreign investment were clear about the approval process for investment projects, and so the Egyptian bureaucracy applied it strictly, as it felt bound to do. The process of approving foreign investment proposal would become easier for investors only with the adoption of new regulations that abolished the old requirements and enabled the Egyptian bureaucracy to facilitate approvals.

Laws and regulations have the beneficial goals of seeking to provide for the impartial functioning of the bureaucracy, to guard against arbitrary action, and to protect the interests of the public. But at the same time, they have the disadvantage of causing rigidity, inflexibility, and delay in the operations and decisions of the bureaucracy. So even if a political leader like Roosevelt or Sadat seeks to institute a new policy, that leader will have to struggle with and perhaps in the end be stymied by established rules and norms that may run counter to the new policy. By contrast, despite the resistance of "corporate culture," a new CEO of a corporation with a new vision and strategy for the company will have much less trouble with a company's existing operating policies and will be much more effective at influencing change in those policies than a new leader in a political system.

Constraint #2: Constituents

Just because a particular government department or agency has a monopoly over what you are seeking in your negotiation does not mean that department or agency is omnipotent. Inevitably, that department or agency depends on some constituency for resources and support, and that constituency can therefore influence the way the particular government department or agency behaves. Depending on the country, state, or locality, government departments and officials rely on a wide variety of constituents and supporters—political parties, labor unions, the military, the media, and civic organizations—from which they derive power and authority. So, in negotiating with any government department, you need to try to understand its particular constituents and the levers they command to influence government action.

The key constituents of a government department are not always readily apparent. Like cultures, each of the world's governmental systems is distinct and different. The French government does not make policy the way the German government does. The laws and court procedures of India are distinct from those of England, even though India was part of the British Empire for many years and today retains the English common law tradition. And an American executive cannot assume that governments abroad work the way the U.S. government does at home. We are therefore tempted to think that government and bureaucratic decision-making is some kind of a mysterious black box, whose workings are difficult if not impossible for an outsider to fathom. One way of beginning to understand them is to look to the constituents and supporters of these agencies in order to understand the influence that they have on the government department in question.

The Constituents of Defense

Raytheon, a major U.S. defense contractor, learned this lesson several years ago when it tried to put together a consortium of European companies to produce for NATO a weapons system that it had already built successfully for the U.S. military. Knowing the capabilities of various European firms, Raytheon selected those it thought would do the best job and began negotiating with them. These conversations were abruptly cut short when individual NATO governments told Raytheon that they, not the American manufacturer, would choose the European participants in the consortium. Recognizing political realities, Raytheon ended discussions with the firms it had selected, began negotiations with those chosen by individual governments, and ultimately put together a consortium that successfully produced the weapons systems for NATO.

A few years later, at the urging of the American government, Raytheon sought to produce a version of the same weapons system for Japan. Having learned what it thought was a useful lesson from its earlier experience in Europe, it opened talks directly with the Japanese government, expecting the government to indicate which Japanese companies the U.S. manufacturer was to work with. No such indication was forthcoming. Japanese officials studiously avoided suggesting appropriate Japanese partners. Finally, in a private conversation with a Raytheon senior executive, the Japanese deputy minister of defense made it clear that the U.S. manufacturer, not the Japanese government, should decide on which Japanese companies should participate in producing the weapons system. The reason was that two very powerful Japanese electronics firms were the primary contenders for participation, and the Japanese government did not want to incur the wrath and political antagonism of either one by choosing the other.[7] The Japanese Ministry of Defense needed the continuing support of both of these constituents if it was to preserve its influence, budget, and status within the Japanese government.

In both the European and Japanese cases, the black box of government processed a political decision, but each came out with a different result. In Europe, in matters of national defense and the allocation of contracts among companies in different countries, there was a dominant supplier, often a government or government-financed entity itself, in each country and they each had significant influence over the government departments concerned with the production of weapons systems. In Japan, the government, when faced with two competing Japanese electronics giants, recognized that if it favored one over the other, the losing company through its political and financial clout could "hurt that department badly."

The Lessons of Constituents

What this little story teaches is that in negotiating with governments you should not only learn the rules of government negotiations, you should also seek to understand the constituents and supporters of the department or agency with which you are negotiating and the degree and form of influence that such constituents and supporters exert in the process of government and policymaking. With that knowledge, you will be able to develop more effective strategies and tactics to deal with governments to get what you want. Without that knowledge, the workings of their governments remain a mysterious black box. One of the functions of lobbyists and government affairs experts is to help you obtain that knowledge.

Chrysler used its knowledge of government constituents to good advantage several years ago in negotiations to sell its money-losing plants in the United Kingdom to the British government. It reacted to the government's low initial offer by threatening to liquidate its factories one by one, beginning with a plant located in an important electoral district in Scotland. The British Labour government at the time had a very slim majority and depended on Scotland to maintain its hold on power. In response to Chrysler's threat, Labour leaders in Scotland put strong pressure on the government to keep the plant open. In the end, the government increased its offer significantly and made a deal with Chrysler.[8]

Constraint #3: The Political Imperative

An understanding of interests, both yours and the other side's, is fundamental to success in any negotiation. All negotiators, governmental or private, are driven by their interests. Those interests are often complex. They are personal and organizational. You cannot assume that the interests of the person sitting on the other side of the table are the same as yours or of other persons you have negotiated with in the past. You have to dig deep to uncover those interests, if you hope to engage in productive negotiations.

Because of their special interests, government officials and politicians perceive and act on negotiating issues and problems in ways that are often different from the way private parties would in similar situations. Part of the reason for this is that whereas corporate deal makers usually respond to commercial incentives—the need to make a profit, to increase share price, or to assure a fat bonus for the year—government officials, whether at the local, state, or national levels, respond to "political imperatives"—the need to protect departmental budgets, to preserve areas of authority and "turf," to enhance departmental prestige, and to ward off competition from other governmental departments. All government negotiators are agents, that is, they are negotiating on behalf of the state or its subdivisions, not for themselves. In practice, as agents they also have their own personal and bureaucratic interests to advance and they will certainly do so in their dealings and negotiations. An understanding of these undeclared interests is vital in dealing with any government department.

One of the consequences of the political imperative and the need to satisfy constituents, especially when the department itself will not directly benefit from your negotiation, is to delay negotiations—sometimes indefinitely—when faced with a contentious issue that may negatively affect its political interests. Rather than make a definite decision that will offend one group or another, the negotiating strategy of choice for most officials is to delay until delay itself may prove too costly. Thus the State of New York took six years to make a decision to deny the application of the St. Lawrence Cement Company to build its new plant because the concerned government departments wanted to avoid political attacks from either the plant's supporters or its opponents.[9]

Constraint #4: Operational Norms

Government departments normally operate according to certain norms that one rarely finds in private business.[10] In particular, these norms affect a government department's revenues, resources, and objectives. They not only influence how government departments act, they also affect how they negotiate.

1. *Revenue Norms*. A first important norm concerns departmental revenues. Part of the reason that governments are not influenced by commercial incentives to the same extent as are private sector companies is that government departments, unlike companies, usually cannot retain the commercial and financial benefits of the deals they make. Whereas a company in negotiating with a supplier will increase its earnings by a dollar for every dollar it saves at the negotiating table, a government department that saves a dollar in negotiating with a supplier will not increase its budget by a dollar. Rather, that dollar goes to the general state budget. In fact, the government department may be penalized next year, when its budget is reduced by a dollar because of the dollar it saved the preceding year in its negotiations with you. This may have some perverse effects. For one thing, it often leads to a flurry of negotiating activity as the end of a particular government fiscal year approaches, so that the government will be sure to spend its annual budget. This factor can be used by a private negotiator to its advantage in order to close a deal that it wants.

Government rules that many private firms can take advantage of are those dealing with governmental appropriations. Many government agencies are given a certain amount of budget each year and there is always the threat that if that money is not spent during that fiscal year, they will not receive as much money the next year. Understanding the budgetary cycle of bureaucracies can work to the advantage of private negotiators as deadlines approach. Many times the act of spending money becomes an end in and of itself.

2. ***Resource Allocation Norms.*** The second important operational norm is that most governments are not free to allocate the various factors of production, such as capital, labor, and technology, the way that the managers and negotiators in that department judge best. Whereas private companies will decide whom to hire and whom to fire, and what equipment to buy or not to buy according to their view of that decision's impact on the profitability of their company, government departments often have to make similar decisions according to politically imposed rules. Since government entities in business are usually subsidized by the state treasury and are controlled by government officials, their principal goal may not be the maximization of profit, as is the case with private firms, but the advancement of social and political ends. For example, if a manufacturing joint venture between a U.S. company and a foreign state-owned corporation were to be faced with a decline in demand for its products, the reaction of the U.S. partner might be to lay off workers. However, the state corporation under government control, despite reduced profitability, might reject that solution to prevent an increase in unemployment in the country. In negotiating a transaction, it is often important to recognize and discuss at the table divergences in goals, rather than be surprised by them later on.

3. ***Objectives Norms.*** The third major constraint is that government agencies and departments must pursue the objectives that the legislator has specified for them. They may not pursue the objectives that they themselves judge important. Thus, even if the TVA had internally determined the importance in engaging in regional planning, it would be constrained from pursuing that objective by its mission to build dams as specified in the law. Companies change products and strategies in accordance with the market demands. Government departments and agencies cannot change objectives as easily. When Ford Motor Company realized that the Edsel automobile, which it introduced in 1957, was a loser in the marketplace, it stopped making it—in 1959. Had Ford been a government department, it would probably still be manufacturing Edsels today.[11]

All of these operational norms strongly influence how governments negotiate, and they constitute special challenges for private persons who would seek to deal with governments.

Conclusion: Seven Rules for Evaluating Governments as Negotiating Counterparts

How can you put your new understanding of government powers and constraints to work the next time you are negotiating with a local, state, federal, or foreign government? The following seven rules will enable you to use that knowledge to achieve better outcomes.

Rule #1: As you approach negotiations with any government, recognize that it possesses powers and is subject to constraints different from those to be found in negotiating with private persons and organizations. Then seek to understand how you may incorporate these factors into your negotiating strategies and tactics. As a result of these powers and constraints, government negotiators will often behave differently from their private sector counterparts at the negotiating table.

Rule #2: Keep in mind that the special powers of governments are derived from their:

- Legal monopoly over what you are seeking
- Special legal privileges and immunities
- Role as defender of the public interest
- Special protocols and forms

Rule #3: Remember that governments are also subject to special legal and political constraints in their negotiations with you. These constraints are derived from:

- The rules governing their negotiations
- The constituents upon whom they depend for support

- The political imperatives to which they respond
- The operational norms mandated by their political masters

Rule #4: All governments and their officials jealously guard their authority because authority is what allows them to govern. Never challenge the authority of a government department or agency and avoid any action that might be interpreted as a challenge. Respect and deference should guide all your negotiations with any government.

Rule #5: Learn the rules governing the negotiation process and the protocols and forms expected of you as a non-governmental negotiator. To gain that knowledge, seek the advice of consultants, people in the particular community concerned, and those persons who have had experience in negotiating with a particular governmental unit.

Rule #6: All governments enjoy to a greater or lesser extent certain privileges and immunities. Learn what they are in the case of the particular government with which you are negotiating.

Rule #7: The "public interest" is always an actual or potential factor in any negotiation with any government. It can turn any seemingly bilateral negotiation between you and a government department into a multilateral negotiation involving uninvited members of the public, civic groups, and the media. You should always plan your negotiations accordingly.

• CHAPTER THREE •

Getting Ready to Negotiate with a Government

> "Luck is what happens when preparation meets opportunity."
>
> —SENECA

In 1974, the Ford Foundation decided to set up a field office and launch a development program in Sudan, a poor and vast African nation whose secular government at the time seemed strongly committed to realizing the country's agricultural potential and improving the lives of its people. The Foundation, for whom I had been working in the Middle East for the previous three years, asked me to establish the office and serve as its first representative in the country. A first step in the process was to negotiate with the Sudanese government a "country agreement" that would permit the Ford Foundation to operate in Sudan and that would at the same time grant it certain privileges, including exemption from Sudanese taxes and customs duties. Before I could sit down to talk with the Sudanese, I first had to prepare.

The Two Dimensions of Preparation

The difference between a successful and an unsuccessful negotiation lies all too often in the quality of the parties' preparation.

Negotiators often fail to make an agreement or to derive maximum benefit from their negotiation because one or both sides did not prepare effectively for the encounter. Probably the worst approach to a negotiation is the attitude "Let's hear what the other side has to say and *then* we'll decide how to deal with them." That attitude is like that of a general who leads an army onto the battlefield declaring, "Let's see what they throw at us and then we'll decide how to get organized." While flexibility and openness are certainly useful in a negotiation, it is also important to prepare for any negotiation in a systematic and structured way.

Preparing for a negotiation has two important dimensions, and you must attend to both to give yourself a maximum opportunity for success at the negotiating table. The first dimension is to *prepare yourself*—to give yourself the knowledge, skills, and attitudes to achieve the goals that you are seeking in a particular negotiation. The second dimension is to *prepare the ground*—to take the actions before you actually negotiate that will increase the likelihood of success once you sit down at the negotiating table. Let's first consider how you should prepare yourself and then examine what it takes to prepare the ground for fruitful negotiations.

Seven Steps to Preparing Yourself to Negotiate

Here are seven steps that you should take to prepare yourself for any negotiation.

Step #1: Determine Your Goals and Your Mandate

In preparing for any negotiation, you must first of all determine your goals. What do you want from the negotiation? A clear definition of your negotiating goal will influence to a large extent your strategies and tactics in the negotiation. And when you are negotiating on behalf of someone else, you must determine your principal's goals and clarify your instructions and authority.

Most of the time when we negotiate, in fact, we are negotiating for someone else. In short, most negotiators are *agents*. Executives are agents for their corporations. Diplomats are agents for their governments. Lawyers are agents for their clients. Those corporations, governments, and clients are our *principals*, the organizations and persons for whom we are negotiating and to whom we are responsible. In my negotiations with Sudan, I was an agent for the Ford Foundation. As an agent in a negotiation, you have to determine your principal's *goals* and you have to be assured that you have a mandate to negotiate on your principal's behalf.

Determining Goals

The purpose of any negotiation is to achieve a particular goal. Before you begin to negotiate, you therefore need to understand clearly what that goal is. If you are negotiating for yourself alone, you normally have only one set of goals. If you are negotiating for someone else, you usually have two sets: yours and your principal's.

Our ability as agents to make deals on behalf of somebody else depends first of all on understanding as clearly as possible our principal's goals and interests in the proposed deal. In preparing to negotiate a country agreement in Sudan, I had to get answers to a long list of questions to understand the Ford Foundation's goals: Why fundamentally did we want an office in Sudan? What would be the scope of our activities in that country? What if Sudan wouldn't give us the privileges we were seeking? How badly did we need them? How would any agreement that we made with Sudan affect our operations in other countries? At the time, I listed my questions on a yellow pad and they went on for several pages.

To get answers to these questions, you need to talk to the people in your organization. For example, suppose that your company has decided to negotiate with a city government to buy the site of an abandoned public school on which to build a new factory and that your CEO asks you to conduct the negotiations. Before you can sit down with the representatives of the city, you'll have to conduct lengthy conversations with various departments within your company to determine their interests in the deal. Why does your company want to make this deal? Is outright purchase the only option? What about a long-term lease? What price is your company willing to pay? What are the various financing mechanisms that are acceptable? What side payments and benefits to the community is the company willing to offer the city to sweeten the deal? What continuing access to the land is the company prepared to allow the city after the deal? How does this deal relate to the company's existing businesses? What kinds of services, roads, and other infrastructure will you have to obtain from the city? After you close the deal, what kind of relationship does your company want with the city and the surrounding community?

These are just a few of the questions you will have to ask in order to come to know your company's interests. You need to go through the same process of interest exploration, whether you are negotiating for a group of parents to obtain authorization from the board of education to open a charter school or for a consortium of banks to gain government approval to set up operations in a foreign country. As you conduct these internal explorations, you will see that different departments, different persons, and different units within your organization perceive the ideal agreement in different ways and that their individual bureaucratic interests have to be accommodated to make the deal happen. For example, in your negotiation to buy city land, the finance department will go along only if the city will provide part of the financing for the purchase and the engineering group will accept it only if there are no environmental problems at the site. Even if certain departments don't have the clout to kill the deal, remember that if you ignore their concerns they can still make implementation of the transaction difficult after you sign the contract.

Securing and Maintaining Your Mandate

To negotiate on behalf of other persons or organizations, you need a *mandate* from those persons—an authorization to act for them. That mandate might include the legal authority to sign a contract, but in most cases it will take the form of negotiating instructions about the kinds of deals that you may explore and perhaps tentatively agree to at the negotiating table. An agent may have very limited legal authority to bind a principal, but may have a broad mandate to explore a wide variety of possibilities. For example, in negotiating many major transactions, such as mergers, joint ventures, or direct foreign investments, both sides understand at the start that anything agreed upon at the negotiating table will have no binding effect until approved by their respective companies. On the other hand, the negotiators' instructions in those same negotiations may be sufficiently broad and clear to give assurance to all sides that whatever the negotiators agree to has a strong likelihood of acceptance back home.

Your mandate is crucial to your ability to negotiate for two important reasons. First, the other side's belief that you have a mandate means that they will negotiate with you seriously as a representative of your organization. Remember, throughout their dealings with you, an unspoken question is always on their minds: Will you be able to deliver? In many types of negotiations with governments, you may have to present documentary proof of your mandate before government officials will talk to you seriously. Second, the existence of a mandate gives you assurance of being able to cause your organization to accept any agreement that you *do* negotiate.

A negotiator's mandate is not simply handed down from on high like the stone tablets bearing the Ten Commandments. Nor does it automatically come with your position or title. In most organizations, a mandate to conduct important external negotiations is the product of an often lengthy *internal* negotiation. For example, to develop a mandate for its executives to negotiate with an Indian state government to construct a power plant in India, a U.S. energy company needed to conduct negotiations among a variety of internal departments—including finance, engineering, and legal, among others—in order to arrive at a common position on such important factors as the minimum acceptable rate of return on the project, the nature of required legal guarantees, and the types of technology that the company would be willing to transfer to India. So just because your CEO told you to negotiate the purchase of city land doesn't mean that you have a strong mandate to do the deal. You will secure a strong mandate only after conducting internal negotiations with all necessary departments within your organization.

In determining an agent's negotiating authority and instructions, agents themselves often play a key role as advisors to their principals.[1] One of the reasons why principals use agents in a negotiation is because of the agent's expertise, and that expertise can allow negotiators to guide the formulation of their authority and instructions. For example, in trying to determine a maximum amount to be obtained from a negotiation, a principal may ask an agent's advice: "How much do you think we can get?" In other cases, when a principal's stated demands are extreme, an agent may have to deflate them by referring to the prevailing standards in a specific area of business as not justifying the principal's expectations. So if a CEO of an energy company wants to instruct a negotiator to obtain a minimum rate of return of 30 percent on the electrical generating station in India, the negotiator might advise the CEO that no Indian government has ever approved a project with that high a rate of return and that, in the negotiator's opinion, starting with such a high demand will not only meet quick rejection but will also sour relations permanently between the Indian government and the company.

No mandate is permanent. A negotiator may gain a mandate to represent other organizations or individuals but lose it later on. You can lose your mandate through your own actions or through the actions and events of others. To maintain your mandate, you must be alert to factors that may damage it. You should also keep key members of your principal's organization informed of your external negotiations and, in appropriate cases, you may actually want to involve them in the process.

To a large extent, your mandate depends not on your position and title but on the nature of your relationships with the people you work with. In this respect, negotiators may play a variety of roles. Some are just "good soldiers," who merely carry out the orders of the people they represent and rarely go beyond them without first checking with their principals. Others are "architects," who after gaining a basic idea of the interests and aspirations of their principals, set out to design a deal through their negotiations with the other side, confident that they will be able to convince their principals to accept it. Whether you can play the good soldier or the good architect will often depend on the strength of your relationships with key persons and departments in your organization. Involving other members of the organization as part of your negotiating team can help to assure and strengthen your mandate. Their participation may serve to assure their departments that your actions in the negotiation are not harming their departments' interests.

Your organization's willingness to grant and allow you to retain a mandate also depends to a large extent on its understanding of the special context in which you operate as a negotiator. Because you have been negotiating with governments in Kansas City or Kuala Lumpur, you have gained a special understanding of the culture, governmental policies, and bureaucratic traditions of those places and have shaped your transactions accordingly. Those same cultures, policies, and traditions may seem a mystery at best or totally unreasonable at worst to your colleagues in the home office. They may therefore resist or oppose the deals you have made, and perhaps even accuse you of "going native" or "selling out to the other side." As a negotiator, it is therefore important to see one of your permanent functions as continually educating key individuals in your organizations about the special needs and challenges of your external negotiations. You may wage your educational campaign in a variety of ways. You might provide key individuals with regular reports on local conditions. You might keep them informed of similar deals being made in those places by your competitors. You might arrange visits to your home offices for key colleagues and counterparts from the field. And finally you might seek to persuade your superiors and key colleagues to travel with you periodically to the sites in which you are working so that they might learn firsthand the nature of local conditions and meet face-to-face with local persons who are important to your company's business.

Step #2: Organize Your Team

The negotiation of a major transaction with a government is usually the work of a team, rather than one individual. Some members of the team sit at the negotiating table. Others remain in the background but nevertheless support the negotiators at the table. Preparation for the negotiation requires that you create a team having the skills and knowledge necessary to succeed in the talks. The team members then need to prepare together and to develop a coordinated plan of action. Here are a few suggestions to facilitate that process.

- Choose the right team.
- Prepare for the negotiation well in advance.
- Agree on a single spokesperson.
- Allocate specific functions and tasks among team members.
- Select an appropriate interpreter.

Let's take a closer look at each of these suggestions.

Choosing the Right Team

The wrong people at the table can kill a deal, no matter how good it looks. Skilled and prepared negotiators, on the other hand, can turn a bad situation around. It is therefore important to select and prepare the negotiating team with care. Consider carefully the size and composition of your team. The size and expertise of the team will depend on the nature of the transaction and the kind of government you are dealing with. Given the fact that any significant negotiations with a government always have important public consequences, people who can understand the politics of government negotiations and who know how to communicate with the public are important elements in any negotiating team.

Preparing in Advance

Negotiators should prepare well in advance as a team, rather than as individuals who come together for the first time to talk about a proposed deal on the plane taking them to the site of the negotiations. To facilitate coordination and communication among the team members, you may want to establish a space within a secure website where various documents related to the negotiation can be stored for consultation over the Internet. As part of their preparation, team members might engage in simulated negotiations and role-play to anticipate the situations they expect to meet.

Agreeing on a Single Spokesperson

The effectiveness of a negotiating team can be severely diminished when more than one person speaks on its behalf. Several voices give several messages, no matter how "in synch" they try to be. This situation confuses the other side and ultimately may lead it to question your side's credibility. Note, however, that the spokesperson need not be the team leader. While a team usually consists of specialists and technicians, the team leader should be a generalist with a broad vision, a person who can integrate the various technical requirements into a broad concept or premise that will become the basis for the deal. In one negotiation several years ago between an American construction company and a Turkish public-sector corporation for a contract to build a dam, both teams consisted only of specialists. Neither had a generalist. As a result, the technicians on each side argued about technical points. No one was capable of developing a general framework for the deal, so the talks ended after a week of fruitless bickering.

Allocating Specific Functions and Tasks

To smooth the negotiation, specific team members should be given definite tasks relating to the negotiation process, including note taking, transportation arrangements, communicating with the home office, and arranging for an interpreter when negotiations will be conducted in more than one language.

Selecting an Appropriate Interpreter

If you are negotiating with a foreign government, you may have to negotiate through an interpreter. In that case, your team should hire its own interpreter. Except in cases where special reasons for trust exist, do not rely on the other side's interpreter unless someone on your team understands the language and can check the translation. Before hiring an interpreter, try to determine the individual's skill and experience from independent reliable sources. Before negotiations actually begin, meet with your interpreter to explain the nature of the transaction you are trying to make. An interpreter may be an expert in languages but will need to be briefed on the nature of the technical and business issues likely to arise during the talks. You should also explain what you want in the way of translation and why you want it. For example, if you want a word for word translation rather than a summary, make your requirements clear. In selecting an interpreter, guard against individuals who, because of personal interest or ego, try to take control of the negotiation or slant it in a particular way. This risk may be present if the interpreter also works as a middleman, agent, or business consultant. On the other hand, a skilled and knowledgeable interpreter can also help you to understand the culture, politics, and bureaucratic traditions of the country in which you are trying to make a deal.

Step #3: Research the Other Side

Effective preparation requires not only knowing as much as possible about the deal that you hope to make but also knowing as much as possible about the *government you hope to make it with*—before you get to the negotiating table. To do this, you need to engage in some intensive research. For example, before flying to Cameroon in West Africa to negotiate a deal with its government to build a pipeline, you should try to learn as much as possible about Cameroon's history, economy, political system, culture, and relationships with its neighbors. You need to engage in the same kind of research before driving down to your local city hall to apply for a permit to build an extension to your home. This vital knowledge will come not only from books, articles, and online sources, but also from talking to people who know the Cameroon environment or who have already dealt with the office in your city hall that issues building permits. In this regard, depending on the size of the deal, you may want to engage a consultant, advisor, or lawyer to assist in your preparations. In view of the fact that any negotiation with a government often involves members of the public, your preparatory research should also try to identify the groups that may oppose or endorse your goals in the negotiation. In short, try to anticipate both sources of opposition and sources of support.

A Lady or a Tiger?

Before undertaking to negotiate a country agreement for the Ford Foundation with Sudan, I first had to figure out with whom I should negotiate to obtain it. Should I talk to the Ministry of Finance since it dealt with tax matters? What about the Ministry of Education, since so many of the Foundation's projects related to education? How about the Ministry of Agriculture, since we planned to provide important support for agricultural research? No law or regulation specifically told me where to go and whom to see. This would be the first time that a foreign private foundation was to set up an office in the country.

Opening moves are important in any negotiation, and this opening move—deciding which ministry to approach—seemed particularly important. Since no other foreign foundations had offices in the country, the ministry that I chose to talk with first would certainly assert its authority over Foundation operations. But would that ministry be a support or an impediment to our work? And if I chose a ministry that turned out to be an impediment, it would be difficult to leave its embrace and try to find a friendlier government department. In a sense, my situation was similar to the old short story "The Lady and the Tiger," by Frank Stockton, which told of an ancient form of trial in which the accused person was marched into an arena where he faced a structure with two doors and was told to open one of them. Behind one door was a lady who would welcome him; behind the other was a tiger that would tear him to pieces. It was clearly important to know what lay behind the ministry door I tried to open. Would I find a negotiator receptive to my proposal and requests or one who would give me a hard time from the moment I stepped into his office?

Before choosing to open the door of a particular ministry, I spent time talking to Sudanese friends, institutions that the Foundation was supporting, aid agencies operating in the country, diplomats who had experience dealing with the Sudanese government, and Sudanese government officials whom I knew. It soon became clear that the ministries of the Sudanese government, like the departments of any government, each had their own separate culture, approaches, and methods of operation. The Sudanese government was definitely not a monolith. Some ministries were more powerful than others. Some were open to foreigners while others were more suspicious. Some were flexible in facing new situations while others were hidebound. A consensus about a negotiation strategy began to emerge. Avoid the Ministry of Education. Stay away from the Ministry of Finance at all costs. Talk to the office in the Ministry of Foreign Affairs, which is responsible for relating to foreign development agencies working in the country.

Step #4: Determine Options

A critical step in preparing to negotiate is to determine options—yours and theirs. Your options fall into two categories: the options that you have in the event that negotiations fail and the options that you are willing to explore with the other side as a basis for the deal.

Best Option in Case of Failure

While determining what you will do if you do not make a deal may seem defeatist, it is nonetheless an important part of your preparation. In their book *Getting to YES*, Fisher, Ury, and Patton stress the importance of defining your Best Alternative to a Negotiated Agreement, knowing your BATNA.[2] Determining your best alternative to a deal has several benefits.

First, it gives you a standard against which to measure any proposal that the other side puts forward. Obviously, you do not want to accept any option at the negotiating table that is worse than what you can obtain elsewhere.

Second, knowing your best alternative to the transaction will often help to build your confidence at the negotiating table. Sometimes it may be possible to improve your best alternative to the deal, thereby increasing your confidence and negotiating power even more. Indeed, the power that negotiators feel at the negotiating table is often directly proportional to how good they judge their best alternative to the deal.

Third, if your alternative is particularly good, you may want to let the other side know it in hopes that it will persuade them to make a deal with you. For example, in the negotiations between Daimler-Benz and Chrysler over their proposed merger, Jürgen

Schrempp, chairman of Daimler-Benz, told Robert Eaton, chairman of Chrysler, that Daimler-Benz had also held talks with the Ford Motor Company about a possible merger. Although Schrempp was not particularly attracted to this option since it meant that Daimler-Benz would be dominated by Ford, he nonetheless revealed it to Eaton as a way of saying that if Chrysler, which had no other potential merger partner, did not make a deal with Daimler-Benz, Daimler-Benz would merge with Ford and Chrysler would be left with no one, a situation that Chrysler feared in an industry marked by overcapacity and increasing competition, an industry in which only the larger automakers would survive. By revealing Daimler-Benz's BATNA, Schrempp moved Eaton toward the DaimlerChrysler merger.[3]

Options for Success

Your preparation should also try to estimate the options available to the other side, an exercise that requires you to put yourself in the place of your counterpart. Sometimes, when faced with adversaries that seem overwhelmingly powerful, a careful analysis of their options, particularly their BATNAs, may reveal that they are not as powerful as they first appear. In the preparation phase, you can only estimate the other side's options. Later, at the negotiating table, you may learn much more about their available options.

You also need to think hard about the various agreement options that will allow you to attain your goals in the negotiation. To pursue that exercise, you first need to understand the interests of the parties at the negotiating table.

Step #5: Define Your Interests and Think About Theirs

Individuals, organizations, and governments engage in negotiations in order to satisfy their interests. It is therefore important to define your interests clearly before you arrive at the negotiating table. We sometimes formulate positions without thinking hard about the interests that shape and drive those positions. For example, before beginning negotiations with a potential new supplier in Malaysia, you need to have clearly in mind *why* you are seeking a new supplier in Malaysia. Is it to lower costs? Is it to avoid overdependence on your current supplier in Dallas? Is it to develop a foothold in Southeast Asia? Is it to learn about the Malaysian market? If your interests are all of the above, then you should prioritize those interests to determine which are more important and which are less important to your business. The nature of those interests will determine the proposals you put forward and the ultimate deal you are willing to accept. For instance, if developing a foothold in Southeast Asia and diversifying suppliers are primary interests, you might be more flexible on pricing than if your primary interest was simply to obtain components as cheaply as possible.

In addition to clarifying your interests as part of preparing to negotiate, you should also think about the other side's interests. Obviously, you will learn more about their interests at the negotiating table, but you ought also to try to estimate the interests that will be driving your counterpart once you sit down to negotiate. For example, if you are planning to negotiate to buy that abandoned school from the city, you should think about the interests of the city government and the local school board in the deal. The city's interests will certainly include obtaining as much money has possible for the property, relief from the financial obligations of maintaining property that they are not using, assurance that the ultimate use of the land by your company will not have negative effects on the community and will not cause an adverse public reaction, and the creation of new jobs and new taxes that your company's new factory will provide. Having identified possible interests, one of your goals at the negotiating table will be to determine how the city prioritizes those interests. If new jobs and new taxes are their top priority, then perhaps the city negotiators will be less insistent on a high price for the property than they would otherwise.

In contemplating interests, you should remember that you will be negotiating with an agent of the government with which you are trying to make a deal. Agents usually pursue their own interests as well as those of their principals. In short, they may have a dual agenda. In its most extreme form, as we saw in Chapter 1, an agent's pursuit of personal interests can lead to demands for bribes and other forms of corruption. As you prepare for deal making, you should contemplate the possibility of requests for corrupt payments and develop strategies and tactics to deal with them.

Coping with Corrupt Interests

The subject of government corruption is complex, and a full treatment is beyond the scope of this book. Its potential to affect a negotiation is influenced by a variety of intricate factors, including the legal or business traditions of the country or industry concerned, the strength of the bureaucracy with which you are dealing, the nature of the persons sitting across the table from you, and your company's own internal policies, culture, and controls, to mention just a few. In nearly all countries, the payment of a bribe to a government official to secure a favorable contract or action in a negotiation is a crime by law; however, the readiness of a particular legal system to enforce those laws varies from country to country, from state to state, and even from town to town. Even if you are negotiating in a country with weak enforcement of anti-bribery laws, you do well to remember that the U.S. Foreign Corrupt Practices Act imposes severe penalties on U.S. companies and persons who pay bribes to foreign officials. Moreover, indulging in bribery has a corrosive effect on your own company and employees, damages your reputation with business associates and the public, and can lead to other types of financial losses.

So, how should you protect yourself against the demands of a corrupt official in your negotiations with government? Although no foolproof protection exists, the following suggestions may help you cope with corruption in your government negotiations.

1. Work to understand the nature of the laws and institutions affecting corrupt payments in the country or area in which you are negotiating and discuss them with your team as part of your preparation.
2. If your company has prepared a code of business ethics or similar document, provide it to the other side as part of the introductory material you ordinarily furnish before or at

the beginning of negotiations. When introducing your company to a governmental unit, you might review that statement in some detail.

3. Develop a strong relationship with a reputable and honest local individual or organization in the area. Often that person or organization has learned how to resist corruption and can advise you on whom to contact in order to counter the demands of a corrupt local official for bribes.

4. If you are approached for a bribe, explain that while you have great respect for your counterpart, you risk prosecution under the Foreign Corrupt Practices Act if you make corrupt payments. When a West African minister during a break in a negotiating session poetically told an American executive that the minister was "the first tree in the forest and needed water," the American replied in friendly but blunt terms: "If I pay you, I'll go to jail. And since you are my friend, I know you don't want that to happen."

5. Try to deflect a demand for a bribe by making a donation or providing a service that benefits the country or the local community. Your company might build a playground for a school or a dispensary for a village, allowing the officials with whom you have been negotiating to take full credit for persuading you to make this gift. Your company might also sponsor free cultural events such as an art exhibit, a play, or a rock concert. If you choose to go this route, you must be absolutely sure that the payments you make do indeed go to finance these charitable and social activities, not to line the pockets of local officials.

6. If corruption is pervasive within an organization with which you are negotiating, you may have no other option than to walk away from the deal. If corruption is not pervasive, you might attempt to involve in the negotiation process persons or departments that are not corrupt with the hope that their presence will serve to control the behavior of negotiators seeking a bribe. In negotiating a long-term sales contract with a manufacturer's representative who is signaling the need for a payoff, you might stress your concerns over technology or quality control and ask that appropriate members of the company's engineering division

participate in the discussions. Another approach is to build a channel of communication at another, you might hope, higher level, then use that channel to persuade the company of the benefits of dealing with you.
7. Recognize that in many cultures gifts are an essential part of building relationships between persons and groups. Not all such gifts are necessarily corrupt or equivalent to bribes. To reject abruptly and moralistically any suggested request for a gift may be interpreted as a rejection of the relationship that the other side considers necessary for doing business with you. Try to set a policy as to the kind of gifts you are prepared to give that are consistent with the law and with your own company's business ethics.
8. Finally, remember that efforts to satisfy the personal interests of your counterparts across the negotiating table are not always illegal or unethical. Their desire for your respect, for favorable standing in the eyes of their superiors, and for positive recognition from colleagues in their organizations are personal interests that you should recognize and in appropriate ways help to satisfy as a means to pursue your company's interests in the negotiation. For example, it never hurts to acknowledge the strong preparation of the other side or to thank them for their gracious hospitality. And if the lead negotiator on the other side is having difficulty understanding the financial technicalities of the deal you are proposing, you may want to explain them in a private conversation rather than to lecture him in detail in front of his colleagues.

Step #6: Identify the Issues

Your preparation needs to determine the precise issues that will arise during the course of the negotiations. An "issue" in this context means a subject of discussion about which the other side may have questions or over which there may be differences in viewpoint between the two sides. For example, in preparing for my negotiations with the Sudanese government, I felt fairly certain that the nature and scope of the tax and customs exemptions that the Ford Foundation was seeking would be an issue in the discussions.

Some issues, such as those relating to price, closing date, methods of payment, and performance specifications, will be obvious. Others may be less apparent. To understand the issues that may be important to the other side, it is helpful to put yourself in their place or to assign a member of your team to play the role of a negotiator for the other side. Just as a devil's advocate helps a lawyer prepare for litigation, a devil's negotiator can help you get ready for a negotiation with a government.

From their perspective, issues may be apparent that were not evident when you looked at the deal only from your vantage point. For example, in preparing to negotiate to establish a power plant in India to sell electricity to a state public utility, looking at the deal from the Indian point of view and particularly considering the country's traditional skepticism toward foreign investment may reveal that your lack of an Indian equity partner in the power project is likely to become a significant issue when you actually begin negotiations with the Indian government. In addition, whenever you negotiate with a government, it is also important to put yourself in the place of the unseen but ever present potential party to the negotiations: the public. What issues will the public raise about your negotiations and how will you deal with them? The St. Lawrence Cement Company seemed totally surprised by the public opposition to its plan to build a $300 million coal-fired cement plant in the Hudson Valley, a clear indication that in its preparation to negotiate with the seventeen local, state, and federal government agencies to obtain the necessary approvals, it did not fully consider the public's interest and the issues that various groups would raise about the plant's impact on the natural environment.

Once you have identified the issues that may be raised in the negotiations, you should prepare yourself to answer them. For example, knowing that the Sudanese negotiating team would raise questions about our request for tax and customs exemptions, I informed myself about the nature of tax and customs exemptions that the Ford Foundation had secured from other countries.

Step #7: Formulate Mutually Beneficial Proposals in Advance

Before arriving at the negotiating table, you should prepare proposals that seem to meet the interests of both sides and could be a basis for an agreement. For example, in negotiating with the U.S. Federal Trade Commission and the European Union Competition Directorate General in 2000 to obtain approval of their merger, AOL and Time Warner formulated possible options as to what they would divest in order to win the blessing of the two governmental agencies. After any divestment, the merged entity would still have to yield the revenues that would make the merger advantageous; that is, the value of the merged entity had to be worth more than the value of AOL and Time Warner separately. In its discussions with the European authorities, AOL–Time Warner agreed to drop Time Warner's proposed acquisition of EMI (a large British music company) to prove to the European Commission that it had no intention of dominating online music distribution. AOL–Time Warner anticipated the interests and concerns of the authorities on both continents and developed proposals in advance to meet them. As a result, both the United States and the European Union approved the merger.[4]

Having carefully considered your own and the other side's interests, as well as your options and theirs, you may want to prepare a draft of the agreement that you hope to achieve. Securing agreement to your draft by your organization or principal can also be a way of securing your mandate and, as we shall see in Chapter 6, it can be a means of influencing the other side—a negotiation power tool once you sit down to talk.

Phases of the Negotiation Process

Being ready to negotiate not only means that you have prepared yourself but also, like a gardener who has readied the soil before planting, that you have prepared the ground for negotiations by taking all the necessary preliminary actions that will facilitate your success once you sit down at the negotiating table. To prepare the ground for negotiation, you must first fully understand the nature of negotiation as a process.

Like other processes, negotiations tend to go through distinct phases. The effective negotiator understands those phases and recognizes that each phase calls for special skills, approaches, and resources. There are three basic phases in any negotiation: prenegotiation, conceptualization, and detail arrangement.

Phase One: Prenegotiation

In the first phase, which can be called prenegotiation, the parties to a potential deal determine whether they want to negotiate at all and, if so, what they will talk about, and how, when, and where they will do it. Much prenegotiation may happen in letters, telephone calls, and faxes even before the parties sit down together, but it may continue for many meetings thereafter. To take an illustration from diplomacy, despite years of contacts between the Arabs and the Israelis during their long conflict, the parties remained stalled in the prenegotiation phase until they decided to go to the Madrid Conference in 1991 to begin substantive discussions as a result of the Gulf War and U.S. diplomacy.

In your own negotiations with government, you should use the prenegotiation phase to learn more about the government office you will be dealing with, the officials you will be talking to, and the potential concerns they may have about what you are asking for. Information gathering and efforts to evaluate each other characterize the prenegotiation phase. Prenegotiation is also a time when you set the stage for the negotiations that are to take place. For example, if you are planning to ask the planning department for a special variance to allow you to build that motorcycle track, you may use the prenegotiation phase to sound them out about past cases, possible obstacles, and even to engage in unofficial brainstorming about possible solutions. The prenegotiation phase ends when both sides make a decision to negotiate a deal together, or when one informs the other, directly or indirectly, that it no longer wishes to continue discussions. If the parties do decide to enter into negotiations, their transition to the next stage of deal making may be evidenced by making an agenda for their talks and even signing a confidentiality agreement in which they promise not to divulge information that is exchanged during their substantive discussions.

Many American negotiators do not devote the time and attentions required by the prenegotiation phase. They want to "dispense with the preliminaries" and to "get down to cases." Negotiators from other countries view prenegotiation as an essential foundation to any relationship; consequently they recognize the need to conduct prenegotiation with care before actually making a decision to undertake substantive negotiations.

Phase Two: Conceptualization

In the second phase of the process, which might be called conceptualization, the parties seek to agree on a basic concept or premise upon which to build their deal. They attempt to establish the fundamental principles that will govern the transaction or agreement they are trying to make. Even if the parties have agreed on the basic nature of their transaction, they will then need to find an acceptable formula for its structure. In one case involving the renegotiation of a long-term contract for the sale at a fixed price of electricity between a state power company in Ghana and a foreign-owned aluminum smelter, the parties, who were stymied on the question of price, only made progress when they agreed on the principle that the price of electricity under the contract would be "linked to the international price of energy."[5] Often the concept or underlying principle, once agreed upon, becomes encapsulated in a terse slogan or label. For example, in the Camp David negotiations between Egypt and Israel over the return of the Sinai, the basic concept of the deal was "land for security." And in the talks between China and the United Kingdom over the reversion of Hong Kong, the principle was "one country, two systems."

The conceptualization phase of negotiations is marked by the definition of the parties' interests, the advancement of proposals and counterproposals, and the exploration of options. The creativity of negotiators comes into play, as they seek to shape a basic concept and to find the precepts for an agreement that will allow both sides to satisfy their interests. Once the parties have agreed on a concept, they may sign a letter of intent or similar document to record their understanding.

Phase Three: Detail Arrangement

The final phase is devoted to working out the details and implications of the agreed-upon concept. This phase relies heavily on technical expertise as the parties explore the problems of implementation. Here, negotiators come to understand the full meaning of the old saying "the devil is in the details." For example, it is one thing to agree with a state power company that the price of electricity should be linked to the international price of energy, but it is quite another to turn that into a formula for an effective pricing system that can be accurately and efficiently applied day-to-day throughout the life of the deal. Similarly, in negotiating to gain city approval to build a shopping center, it is one thing to gain general approval for the project but it is quite another to reach agreement on all the details from the design of the parking lot to the height of the roof line.

No negotiation is as neat and simple as this three-phase model suggests.[6] In the heat of discussion, the precise boundaries between the different phases may be unclear. Sometimes when the parties are unable to find an acceptable concept, they may try to agree on certain details in order to build confidence in one another and to give their talks the appearance, and perhaps the reality, of having momentum.

Six Ways to Prepare the Ground During Prenegotiation

To prepare the ground for actual negotiations, you should use prenegotiation to maximum advantage. Prenegotiation is important for information gathering, for developing strategies, and planning tactics, but you can also use it to prepare the ground through action. The basic questions you should ask are: What actions can I take before negotiations start that will increase the chances for a successful negotiation once we sit down at the table? In negotiating with governments, here are a few important steps that you should consider to prepare the ground for negotiations:

Step #1: Build Productive Relationships with Your Counterparts

Although you have not actually begun to negotiate, you can begin to develop a relationship with your counterparts in early meetings where you get to know one another and perhaps begin to discuss the development of a process that will facilitate negotiations, for example, by agreeing on an agenda and the timing of the talks. In those preliminary discussions, the parties will begin to understand each other's backgrounds and capabilities and a belief may hopefully emerge that they can trust one another. For example, in your negotiation to buy the abandoned school from the city, you will want to try to form a personal connection with your counterparts from the city.

Step #2: Develop Supportive Alliances

Your counterparts in the negotiation are subject to a variety of influences. As we noted in Chapter 2, governmental units have constituents and supporters. If you can develop supporting alliances with these constituents and mobilize them in your cause, they may help to influence your government negotiating counterparts in your favor. For example, before negotiating with the Sudanese Ministry of Foreign Affairs, I asked the heads of various institutions with which the Ford Foundation has been working, such as the University of Khartoum and the Ministry of Agriculture, to endorse the establishment of a Foundation office by personally contacting officials in the Ministry of Foreign Affairs. In your negotiation to purchase that abandoned school, you might try to have the labor union representing your workers or the contractor who will be constructing your new plant put in a good word for your plans with the mayor, the city council, and the city manager.

Step #3: Consult and Inform the Public

In government negotiations that affect the public interest and therefore raise the possibility that the public and civic groups may become involved, it is often useful to prepare the ground for negotiation by informing and consulting with them about your plans. Not only will this direct contact allow you to give them your views on the project and hopefully dispel damaging rumors and unsubstantiated charges, but you may learn about their concerns and thus be in a position to take account of their issues by altering the nature of your project. The St. Lawrence Cement Company did not engage in any meaningful consultation with people in the Hudson Valley before it began its negotiations to obtain government approvals. If it had, it might have been able to reduce the level of opposition to its proposed new plant. This recommendation to consult with the public seems to run counter to the instinct for confidentiality of most business executives. They often hope that by keeping their plans and negotiations confidential they will obtain government approvals before opposition materializes and thus be able to face protestors with a *fait accompli*. This perspective has two flaws. First, no negotiation with a government will stay confidential for very long. Second, even if you obtain government approval, public opposition that develops *after* you receive it may be strong enough to prevent you from undertaking your project, and in that situation you are likely to find the government unwilling to help you.

Step #4: Consult and Inform Key Players

In many negotiations with governments, there are key personalities—politicians, business leaders, and media figures—on the sidelines who can either hurt you or help you. In order to obtain their acquiescence to if not their outright support for your plans and in hopes of preventing them from becoming opponents, you should consult with them about the proposed negotiation before actually sitting down at the bargaining table. So if you are planning to seek the approval of the city planning board to build a hotel, you are well advised to pay a courtesy visit to the city's mayor to explain your plans. For every government negotiation you undertake, you need to identify the key political and civic leaders whom you should consult in order to prepare the ground.

Step #5: Set a Productive Agenda

Setting the right agenda for your negotiations with the government is another important means of preparing the ground for fruitful negotiations. The subjects that are and are not on the agenda to be discussed, the sequence in which topics that are on the agenda will be discussed, and the timing allotted for discussions are all important factors that can either favor or impede the attainment of your goals. It is therefore important that you think hard about the kind of agenda you want and how to get it during your prenegotiation contacts with your government counterparts.

Step #6: Prepare the Environment

Negotiations do not happen in a vacuum. They take place in a specific environment, and the elements of that environment—place, time, surroundings, and people—can profoundly influence the course of discussions. You should think carefully about how these elements may affect your negotiation and how you can manage them to maximize your likelihood of success. While many negotiations with governments take place in government offices, that's not always the case. If you can hold negotiations in another setting, for example in your offices or a neutral location, that factor may facilitate relationship building and the development of a positive view toward you and your proposed action. In 1992–1993, Northwest Airlines effectively prepared the environment in its negotiations with KLM, the Dutch airline, over an alliance of the two firms. Northwest knew that KLM, a much smaller airline, was sensitive about its status, both during the negotiation and in any eventual alliance. To alleviate these fears, Northwest structured every aspect of the negotiation—from the prenegotiation dinner to the meeting of delegations with designated chairmen—as a summit meeting between two equal states. According to one Northwest executive participating in the negotiation, "We used every symbol we could think of to recognize their sovereignty."

Conclusion: Six Rules for Getting Ready to Negotiate with Governments

To get ready to negotiate with any government you need both to prepare yourself and to prepare the ground. To prepare yourself, take the following seven steps:

1. Determine your goals and assure your mandate.
2. Organize your negotiating team.
3. Research the other side.
4. Identify your options and estimate the other side's.
5. Define your interests and speculate on theirs.
6. Identify the issues that are likely to be the subject of discussions.
7. Formulate mutually beneficial options to put on the table at the appropriate time.

Understanding the three phases of negotiation—prenegotiation, conceptualization, detail arrangement—allows you to use the prenegotiation phase to maximum advantage in preparing the ground for negotiations. To maximize your chances of success, here are some rules for action to take *before* you begin negotiations:

Rule #1: Build relationships with your potential counterparts.

Rule #2: Build and mobilize alliances with constituents and others that may influence your counterparts.

Rule #3: Consult with the public in appropriate cases.

Rule #4: Consult with key players on the sidelines.

Rule #5: Set a productive agenda for the negotiation.

Rule #6: Shape a positive negotiating environment.

· CHAPTER FOUR ·

The Myth of the Monolith

How Government Organization Affects Negotiations

> "You will find that the State is the kind of organization which, though it does big things badly, does small things badly, too."
>
> —JOHN KENNETH GALBRAITH

In December 1990 and February 1991, a team of bond traders at Salomon Brothers, then the fifth largest financial firm in the United States, submitted unauthorized bids in the name of clients in a deliberate violation of U.S. Treasury Department rules governing auctions of U.S. government securities. Through this stratagem, the Salomon Brothers bond traders circumvented a recent Treasury rule limiting any firm's bid and award on five-year government notes to no more than 35 percent of the issue. When word of this ploy leaked to the press and the public the following August despite management attempts to cover it up, the Securities and Exchange Commission (SEC), the U.S. Treasury Department, the Justice Department, the Federal Reserve, the Federal Bureau of Investigation, and the Manhattan district attorney all launched criminal investigations. Even worse, the Treasury Department decided to ban Salomon Brothers from participating in Treasury auctions in the future, an action that would end a profitable line of business, cause the loss of important customers, prompt the flight of vital short-term creditors, and seriously—perhaps mortally— damage the company's reputation. Salomon Brothers, it seemed, was about to go down the tubes.

Warren Buffett's Successful Negotiation

With the firm's future clearly in jeopardy, the legendary investor Warren Buffett, a Salomon Brothers director whose firm, Berkshire Hathaway, was the company's largest single shareholder with some $700 million at risk, took over as company chairman on Sunday, August 18, 1991, when top management resigned under pressure. One of the first things Buffett decided he had to do that Sunday, which he later described as "the most important day of my life,"[1] was to somehow persuade the U.S. government to reverse its ban on Salomon Brothers' participation in future government securities auctions.

Despite his wealth and influence, Buffett, like anyone contemplating a negotiation with the government, faced a major challenge in figuring out how to move a massive government organization to take action in his favor. A first step in the process was to find the right governmental unit and, within it, the right person or persons to talk to about his problem. That unit and the persons within it not only had to have the power to change the government's position but also be willing to talk to Buffett. Moreover, that conversation had to happen quickly, preferably that very Sunday afternoon, before word of the ban began filtering into foreign markets, which were scheduled to open within a few hours.

Buffett chose to contact Nicholas Brady, U.S. Secretary of the Treasury, in an effort to lift the ban. Through a series of telephone calls that afternoon, which also involved Gerald Corrigan, president of the New York Federal Reserve Bank, Buffett succeeded in negotiating an agreement with Brady and the Fed that allowed Salomon Brothers to continue to participate in U.S. Treasury auctions for its own account, though not for the account of customers. Secretary Brady announced the change in the Treasury's position, stating that he looked forward to a constructive relationship with Salomon Brothers' new chairman. Buffett's successful negotiation with the U.S. government was an important step in ultimately saving the firm.[2]

Organizational and Personal Dimensions

Buffett's negotiation with Brady had both personal and organizational dimensions. In this respect, it was like all negotiations between a private party and a government department. When you negotiate with governments, the individuals on the other side of the table, whether they are bureaucrats or politicians, are embedded in some form of governmental organization and their role when they are talking to you is ostensibly to represent the interests of that organization. The government official to whom you are talking, like U.S. Treasury Secretary Brady in his negotiation with Buffett, is therefore a representative of that organization and in many cases of the entire government. If you are conducting those discussions on behalf of a company or a private organization, you too are a representative. Thus Buffett, despite his firm's investment in Salomon Brothers, in that negotiation was acting as a representative of Salomon Brothers, seeking to secure a benefit—the privilege of participating in government securities auctions—necessary for the company to stay in business. He was not negotiating on his own behalf. Both Buffett and Brady were therefore acting as organizational representatives in their telephone conversations. Their organizational roles heavily influenced their behavior as negotiators.

At the same time, negotiations by their very nature have to take place between individuals. Despite advances in information and communications technology, no government or other organization can conduct negotiation in any but the simplest transaction except by using a human being to do so. A government negotiator, no matter how powerful, is not a robot. Because negotiations with governments are always conducted by human beings, their individual interests, reputations, abilities, and emotions always intrude to some extent into the negotiation, as do your own. Suppose, for example, that you are negotiating to obtain regulatory approval of a new product from a government agency.

Whether the government negotiator sitting across the table from you is a recent, energetic law school graduate or a tired engineer at the end of his career can have an effect on your negotiation and therefore your ability to get the approval you need.

In the case of the negotiation to save Salomon Brothers, the individual qualities of both Buffett and Brady as persons had an important impact on the process and results of their talks. For one thing, Buffett's solid reputation for business probity and the fact that he and Brady had been acquaintances over the years had the effect of giving him access to Brady on a Sunday afternoon, of causing Brady to take Buffett's concerns and requests seriously, and of assuring Brady that real change would take place at Salomon Brothers under Buffett's leadership.

The negotiation also had certain personal risks for Brady. If further scandals occurred after Brady had modified the Treasury's position, Brady would have been open to severe criticism from the public, the media, and many parts of the government bureaucracy. A similar conversation between another two individuals holding the same organizational positions about the same topic might have reached a very different result because of their very different personal characteristics. For example, if the previous Salomon Brothers Chairman and CEO, John Gutfreund, who had been involved in the cover-up, had stayed on the job and had called Brady in an attempt to change the Treasury Department's decision to suspend Salomon Brothers from government securities auctions, Brady would almost certainly have turned him down flat.

As we can see, then, every negotiation with a government has personal and organizational dimensions. Every government negotiator is influenced by both organizational and individual concerns. In this chapter, we examine primarily the role of organizations in negotiating with governments while affirming the importance of personal characteristics of the negotiators in influencing the results of any government negotiation.

Penetrating City Hall

When we begin a negotiation with a government, we are often struck first of all by government's *physical* manifestations, primarily the buildings in which it is housed. Government buildings, like the U.S. Treasury Department in Washington, D.C., the towering city hall in downtown New York City, and virtually any state house in the United States, are massive, imposing, and sometimes forbidding. They often seem like impenetrable fortresses that both protect their inhabitants—the bureaucrats and politicians inside—and at the same time repel or at least hold off those who would seek to enter without an invitation. That impression created by government architecture is intentional. It is yet another of government's signals to the world, like its protocols, of government power and authority. Indeed, the very message that a building like New York City Hall, a massive pile of masonry, seems to communicate is that "you can't fight city hall, so don't even think about it."

Once inside the building, we are often impressed by the number of people working there, the complexity of tasks they carry out in seemingly mysterious ways, and the intricate, apparently unfathomable relationships they appear to have with each other. A government department or agency to the outsider appears to be a complex, impenetrable monolith. If you are going to be able to get what you want from a government, you will have to penetrate that monolith. To do that, you will have to accomplish three tasks. First, you will have to identify the governmental units that can give you what you want. Second, you will have to find the particular person or persons within that unit who can cause that governmental unit to act in a desired way. And third, you will have to persuade that person or persons to actually sit down and talk meaningfully to you about your problem. The first step is a task of *organizational analysis*, the second is *counterpart selection*, and the third is *counterpart access*. Let's consider each of these challenges in depth.

Organizational Analysis: Finding Your Way Around City Hall

Governments act through many different kinds of organizations: departments, "independent" agencies, boards, commissions, and state corporations, to name just a few. Within those organizational entities, there usually are units with specialized responsibilities. The challenge for the negotiator is to identify the governmental unit that can potentially help and then to find within that organization the right person to negotiate with.

Warren Buffett's Organizational Analysis

Consider the problem that Warren Buffett faced in deciding how to move the U.S. government to change its position on banning Salomon Brothers' participation in government securities auctions. Buffett had to decide which governmental unit to engage in negotiations. Should it be the Treasury Department or some other government department, such as the White House or Congress? If he decided on the U.S. Treasury Department, precisely *where* in the labyrinth of governmental sections, offices, and bureaus should he direct his efforts?

Buffett certainly knew President George H. W. Bush and by virtue of that relationship might have been able to mobilize White House pressure on his behalf. Similarly, Buffett had powerful friends in the U.S. Congress from whom he might have sought help. However, both courses of action, particularly as an initial option, had considerable risks. For one, it might have hardened the Treasury's position and put the U.S. Treasury Secretary in the difficult situation of being caught between the pressure from the White House or Congress and pressure from the Treasury Department bureaucracy. In effect, mobilizing the White House or Congress on his behalf would have been seen as a very public challenge to the Treasury Department's authority. In that situation, most Treasury secretaries and their bureaucracies would have felt themselves bound to defend the authority of the departments they run. A further risk is that when you seek to mobilize third persons on your behalf in disputes with others, you are less able to control their actions than if you yourself are acting alone. For both of these reasons, Buffett wisely chose to deal with the Treasury Department and the Treasury Department alone.

Buffett then had to decide whether to go directly to the Treasury secretary or to seek to engage other parts of that department, for example the Treasury official or unit who had issued the ban in the first place. Buffett probably realized that the likelihood of persuading the official who made the order to rescind it was not high, particularly in a case that had attracted such widespread negative publicity. Any official would be highly sensitive to being seen as backing down under pressure and would probably have resisted forcefully any change in the ban. Moreover, in dealing with that official, Buffett probably would not have been able to use a key negotiating asset that he had if he dealt with Brady: a longstanding, friendly relationship. Buffett therefore chose to engage Brady rather than a high-ranking official of the Treasury in his negotiation. It proved to be the right choice.

Learning the Bureaucracy

In pursing the task of organization analysis for the purpose of launching a negotiation, you need to ask five basic questions:

1. Which department or agency can give me what I want?
2. Which part of that department or agency do I need to engage particularly?
3. What other department or agency needs to be involved in or informed of the negotiation and what is the nature of the relationships among them?
4. Should I talk to them together or separately?
5. If separately, in what sequence should I talk with them?

The answers to these questions are not always self-evident. An effective negotiator must therefore spend time studying government organization and bureaucracy in order to answer these questions. Where do you find the answers? First, governments often produce documents on organization. For example, the structure of virtually any government department or agency is determined by some law, regulation, or rule. Find that basic document and study it. Second, governments often produce organizational manuals to assist the public and other units of the government in dealing with it. Third, try to find persons who may already have dealt with a particular government department and learn their experience. Fourth, in complicated situations you may need to obtain the services of a knowledgeable third party, such as a consultant, lobbyist, or lawyer, to help you navigate through the complexity of governmental organizations. And finally, as you carry out your study of government and bureaucracy, be alert to an important constant of bureaucratic life and how it may affect your negotiation: internal conflict.

Fights Inside City Hall

The impression that government organizations and buildings give is that government is a monolith, a united force of people and resources working closely together in the public interest. The buildings of course are only the outward manifestation of governments. They may symbolize government's power but they are not the source of that power. The source of a government's power is its organization. A government may employ millions of people and have vast amounts of resources at its command, but its ability to use those people and resources to achieve its goals depends on a system of organization. Without organization, government's bureaucrats would sit idly at their desks and government's resources would remain unused in the warehouse.

The German sociologist Max Weber, the founding father of the study of bureaucracies, considered hierarchy, along with rules, a fundamental characteristic of bureaucracy. Hierarchy, the arranging of bureaucratic offices and personnel into a structure, is a form of organization. James Q. Wilson, a modern-day student of bureaucracy, concluded that organization was more than mere hierarchy. Its essence lies in its ability to coordinate effective bureaucratic action. As Wilson wrote, "An organization is not simply, or even principally, a set of boxes, lines, and titles on an organization chart. An organization, in the words of Chester Barnard, is 'a system of consciously coordinated activities or forces of two or more persons.' The most important thing to know is how that coordination is accomplished."[3]

The essence of organization, whether bureaucratic or corporate, is the ability to coordinate activities and forces to achieve specific ends. Effective coordination among government departments allows government to act. Ineffective coordination leads to wasted resources, failed policies, and sometimes governmental paralysis. The failure of the Federal government to aid the victims of Hurricane Katrina on the Gulf Coast was not due to lack of recourses. It was due to lack of coordination. The lack of meaningful coordination between the U.S. Department of Defense and the Department of State has meant that certain American interests abroad have not been effectively advanced. Better coordination between the CIA and the FBI in the form of sharing intelligence might have enabled the U.S. government to defend itself more effectively against the terrorist attacks of September 11, 2001.

What prevents effective coordination among governmental units? The obstacle to coordination is conflict. While government departments like to present the appearance of well-oiled machines to the public, their reality is often the opposite. In fact, government departments are often rife with conflict and struggles for power and resources among government units and within those units among bureaucrats. It is the desire of individual politicians, bureaucrats, departments, and individual agencies to enhance their power that leads to conflict among them and that in turn inhibits coordination and therefore effectiveness.

An important school of bureaucratic studies views bureaucracy through the lens of conflict and considers conflict an important explanatory variable for the way governments behave.[4] So it is important for you as a negotiator with governments to recognize that within the fortress of government buildings like the U.S. Treasury or New York City Hall is constant and unceasing conflict. Neither the Treasury nor City Hall is as monolithic as it would like to appear and usually does appear to the public. Indeed, government's monolithic nature is a myth. It is important for negotiators with governments to understand this fact because it can have significant consequences, both positive and negative, on the conduct and results of their negotiations.

Conflict between departments can prevent the making of decisions that the negotiator is trying to secure. Even if the department you choose to deal with can legally deliver what you want, you may have to negotiate with other governmental units to make the deal effective. Sometimes you have to bring other departments to the bargaining table and make them part of the agreement. At other times, you are better off dealing with them separately, as certain American executives did when negotiating a long-term purchase of natural gas from Algeria. They had to be careful in choosing which Algerian ministries to talk with in order to avoid being caught in fights between the Ministry of Energy and the Ministry of Foreign Affairs.

In the same vein, when I was living in Sudan in the 1970s, potential foreign investors seeking to develop agroindustrial projects, such as a sugar plantation and refinery, sometimes found themselves in the middle of conflict between the Ministry of Agriculture and the Ministry of Industry as to which had control over the undertaking. Because of intense jealousy between the two ministries, investors preferred to deal with each one separately since that approach made each ministry feel that it had primary authority over the project. In other situations, officials seeking to reach agreement will bring into the negotiation other government departments. Thus, U.S. Secretary Brady, aware of the strong negative reaction by Gerald Corrigan, the president of the New York Federal Reserve Bank, to the illegal actions of Salomon Brothers' bond traders and the clout that Corrigan exercised in the financial world, knew that he had to involve Corrigan in the discussions and to obtain the Fed's acquiescence for any change in the ban.

Brady knew that if you leave an important governmental unit out of the negotiation, that omission may kill or at least delay a deal. Much time has to be spent in soothing hurt feelings, and the neglected unit invariably feels the need to be difficult to demonstrate its importance. Leaving an important government unit out of a negotiation is in effect a challenge to its authority—the first mortal sin of government life. It is saying, "This negotiation is none of your concern." Remember, the neglected government department is not likely to come running to the negotiation table just because you belatedly extend an invitation. This reaction to challenged authority is by no means unique to Algerian or Sudanese bureaucrats and officials. American officials at all levels can act in the same way when they believe their authority has been challenged because you apparently have ignored them.

Settling Fights at City Hall

If intragovernmental fights and struggles are a constant phenomenon within bureaucracies, how are those struggles resolved? Often, they are not settled at all but become a permanent feature of bureaucratic life. As a result, a state of bureaucratic dysfunction develops that can have devastating consequences for a society, as did the conflicted relationship between the FBI and the CIA before 9/11. Sometimes, the various departments negotiate a settlement among themselves when they come to realize that a settlement advances their interests more than does persisting conflict. Sometimes, leadership resolves the conflict, as where a department head or political official responsible for a department imposes a solution. In the case of Salomon Brothers being banned from government securities auctions, Buffett knew better than to try to get the Treasury official or department that had made the decision to repeal or reconsider. That approach would have encountered serious resistance. Instead, he went to the Treasury Secretary who had legal authority over those who made the decision. Nonetheless, one can imagine that Brady had to do some serious negotiating of his own within the Treasury Department to obtain acquiescence to his decision.

Have You Found the Right Branch?

Often it is not enough to negotiate with the right government department; you must be sure that you are dealing with the right branch of that department. If you are seeking to negotiate a deal within a unit in a highly decentralized bureaucracy, it may be pointless to try negotiations with the department's head office rather than with the subsidiary itself. On the other hand, in a highly centralized structure, it may be essential to negotiate with or at least gain the acquiescence of the head office.

In one Soviet-era case in which I was involved, high-level officials from a ministry in the Soviet Union on a visit to the United States met with executives of an American organization and strongly urged them to begin negotiating a deal with two institutions under the ministry's control. Shortly after, the ministry sent a formal invitation to the Americans to visit Moscow, and the Soviet embassy in Washington also voiced encouragement. Convinced of Soviet readiness to reach an agreement, the American organization sent a team that I headed to Moscow.

Ministry officials hosted a first meeting between our delegation and the heads of the two institutions under the ministry's control. The two institution heads were polite but cool. They found a "problem" or a "difficulty" for each proposal that we put forward. At the end of the day, nothing had been accomplished. That evening, at a reception, I asked the head of one of the Soviet institutions why the negotiations were going nowhere. He responded that the proposed deal had been dreamed up by the ministry, that he had not been consulted until two days earlier, and that the ministry expected his already constrained budget to finance the agreement—something he refused to do. When I asked about the high-level ministry officials who had been so encouraging, the negotiator dismissed them with a wave of his hand. "Them? They are generals without armies. We've got the facilities and the people. It's our budget, not theirs. If you want to do business, you've got to deal directly with us." In fact, we were able to reach agreement with the two institutions only by gently and politely sidelining the ministry representatives and negotiating a protocol directly with the two institution heads that satisfied the particular concerns of their two institutions, which were theoretically subject to Ministry supervision. So much for the legendary monolithic bureaucracy of the Soviet Union!

Government Interest

Even though you are negotiating a deal only with private parties, that fact does not mean that a government cannot somehow become involved—and that at some point you will also have to negotiate with a governmental unit to make the deal a reality. It is therefore important in negotiating any transaction to understand the position, actual or potential, of relevant governmental units toward the deal, even though they are not sitting at the table. Although markets have replaced government directives in much of the world and pervasive government regulation has yielded to deregulation, few countries, even the most stoutly capitalist, are willing to let private persons and companies make any kind of business deal they want. For example, in 2001, although the U.S. government had approved General Electric's acquisition of Honeywell, the European Union competition authorities rejected it and thereby scuttled the entire deal. Earlier, the same authorities responsible for competition in Europe had approved the AOL–Time Warner merger only on the condition that AOL–Time Warner agree to drop Time Warner's proposed acquisition of EMI, a large British music company, to prove to the European Commission that it had no intention of dominating online music distribution—an eventuality that AOL–Time Warner had prepared for. And of course, the United States itself has numerous special laws and regulations that foreign companies must comply with if they want to do business in this country. So in making any deal, it is wise to make clear to your counterparts during negotiations and to include specifically in any contemplated contract that the agreement is conditioned on securing all appropriate governmental approvals.

If a government senses that a proposed transaction between private parties is not in its interest, it will intervene in the negotiation process or, if a contract has already been signed, take action, as the European competition authorities did, to make its execution difficult if not impossible. Thus, an additional important question for any negotiator is whether the governments of the areas affected by the proposed deal have an interest in the transaction, will permit it to happen, and if so under what conditions they will allow it.

Even more critical is the question of whether adverse public reaction to a business deal will cause a government to intervene. In 2006, when Dubai Ports World, a company controlled by one of the Arabian Gulf states, proposed to take over P & O, an international operator of ports including six in the United States, U.S.

public concern about the deal's potential effect on the country's security led to a negative reaction in Congress and proposed legislation to ban the deal. The furor ended only when Dubai Ports World decided to sell off the U.S. operations.[5]

A careful reading of economic policy statements, related legislation, and national development plans can reveal national priorities and how they may affect private business transactions. Conversations with government officials will indicate how legislation and policy are applied in practice, particularly to the transaction that you are contemplating. Sometimes a country does not seem to have well-defined priorities. Initially, a foreign executive may interpret the lack of stated priorities as a favorable openness by that country to all sorts of business deals and investments by foreign companies. That initial reading often proves wrong. In the economies of scarcity that exist in many countries, priorities that go unstated in relatively good times inevitably emerge in tougher times when governments have to make hard decisions about allocating foreign exchange, energy, raw materials, or even space for freight in an antiquated railroad or port. The discovery of these priorities *after* a foreign company has invested time and money in a transaction can prove costly if a government eventually decides that the deal is not important. In planning any transaction, do not take a government's general statements of economic openness at face value. You need to make your own hard-headed analysis of how the government will react toward your deal in both good times and bad. One important way of getting this information is by talking to local business people with firsthand knowledge of how the government has reacted to economic hard times in the past.

Government at the Table

Once you have determined the nature of government interest in a transaction, you need to consider whether the government should be part of the deal. Should the government be at the negotiating table? The answer to this question depends on the kind of deal you are trying to make, the kind of economy you will have to operate in, and the kind of political system you will have to cope with.

A U.S. auto company faced this problem when it negotiated one of the first joint ventures to produce motor vehicles in China. To operate effectively, the new factory would need a supply of parts, but China at that time had no plants to manufacture them. After the deal was signed and the factory constructed, the U.S. company applied to the Chinese government for foreign exchange to import the parts. The government, which had not signed the joint-venture agreement, felt under no obligation to provide foreign exchange for this purpose. As a result, a period of intense conflict between the government and the U.S. automaker followed. Clearly this was a case in which the government should have been brought to the table at the time the joint venture was being arranged so that the partners could obtain a commitment from the government to provide foreign exchange for the parts.

It is also important to understand how state-owned corporations or agencies with which you are dealing relate to the government itself. For example, most state corporations are supervised by a particular government ministry. A national hotel corporation may be supervised by the ministry of tourism and the national airline may be controlled by the ministry of transport. Are the individual corporations free to contract on their own or must their agreements be approved by the relevant ministry to become effective? If the creditworthiness or reliability of a state corporation is uncertain, you may wish to make a government ministry a party to the deal or to secure its guarantee.

If you want the government to be a party to a deal, be sure that its representatives thoroughly understand your intent and that the contract clearly reflects that fact. In one case that became the subject of much litigation, an investment contract for the development of a resort near the Giza pyramids in Egypt stated that the parties to the deal were the state-owned Egyptian General Organization for Tourism and Hotels (EGOTH) and a foreign company. At the closing, the negotiators for the foreign company insisted that the Egyptian minister of tourism also sign the agreement on behalf of the Egyptian government. Eventually the minister did sign, adding the words "approved, agreed, and ratified." Three years later the Egyptian government summarily canceled the contract in the face of a public outcry against the resort project. The foreign investor sued both the Egyptian government and EGOTH in arbitration. Throughout the litigation, which languished for fifteen years in various tribunals and courts, the Egyptian government argued that the minister had not signed as a *party* to the contract but only as the *supervising authority* over the hotel corporation: he was merely approving the hotel organization's participation in the deal. Had the original contract made it clear that the Egyptian government was a party to the contract, the government would not have had a basis for resisting the claim.

Counterpart Selection: Finding the Right Person to Talk To

Once you have identified the right governmental units to deal with you then have to find the right person within that unit to talk to. The right person is the individual who can cause that unit to give you what you want. For example, to reverse the Treasury ban against Salomon Brothers, Warren Buffett chose to talk to Secretary of the Treasury Brady alone.

Various considerations led him to that choice: the fact that the bureaucracy having made a ruling would resist changing it; the fact that he knew Brady and that Brady knew him; the fact that Brady had the power to overrule the ban if solid reasons could be advanced; the fact that Buffett's assumption of the chairmanship of Salomon Brothers and his reforms gave Brady new justification that was not present at the time the original ban was made; the fact that banning a traditionally important participant like Salomon Brothers from Treasury auctions might have the perverse effect of reducing competition in the auctions and thereby result in the U.S. government having to pay more for its money—these were all factors that probably led Buffett to go directly to Brady. Trying to use the White House or Congress to resolve the problem would certainly have led to delay, endless consultations and meetings, and a defensive Treasury bureaucracy, which might have been able to ally Brady with its original position.

The Government Class Struggle

The word "government" encompasses a vast array of institutions and individuals. For the negotiator, a crucial step is to decide with whom to negotiate in order to obtain what he or she wants. If the ultimate goal is to secure a desired agreement from a governmental unit, an important first step is to determine *who* in government you need to negotiate to obtain that agreement. You may of course decide that you will have to negotiate with more than one person and that several individuals representing diverse aspects of government have to be involved in one way or another in the negotiation.

Within the organization of government, there are potentially three classes of individuals with whom you may negotiate to solve your problem: elected politicians, political appointees, and members of the government's more or less permanent bureaucracy. They are three distinct classes because each has its own interests to advance, each has different powers and responsibilities, and the members of each come to their positions in a different way. Equally important, each may behave differently in its negotiations with you. Within each group or class, there is a strong commonality of interests and viewpoints. At the same time, each group constitutes a distinct class with its own interests and outlooks, a class that is in one way or the other in a constant struggle with the other classes. Whether a politician, a political appointee, or a bureaucrat sits on the opposite side of the table from you, you can have an important impact on your negotiation. Let's look at each one briefly.

Elected Politicians as Negotiators

The overriding interest of any politician is being elected in the first place and then being reelected. As a result, any politician—whether a small-town mayor, a state governor, or a congressional representative—will evaluate any proposal in a negotiation in terms of its potential impact, positive or negative, on his or her chances for reelection. Indeed, electoral politics will determine whether a politician will even be willing to meet with you. For example, a few years ago in an effort to establish a federal nuclear waste depository, Congress created a position entitled the "Federal

Nuclear Waste Negotiator" with responsibility for finding an appropriate site in the United States where a depository might be located. Given the general opposition throughout the country to having a nuclear waste depository in their community, you will not be surprised that when the Federal Nuclear Waste Negotiator arrived in a particular locality, no elected official would meet with him or even be seen in the same room.

You therefore need to constantly bear in mind the overriding effect of electoral politics if a politician sits across from you at the negotiating table. He or she will be concerned about the political dimensions of the subject under discussion, no matter how technical, as well as how the negotiation will be viewed by the public and the media. Important factors to consider are when the next elections are to take place and how the politician you are negotiating with evaluates his chances of winning. So if a mayor is in the midst of a tight election fight and the election is next week, she is not likely to agree to authorize a major new shopping mall that has divided the community. And if you are trying to persuade a congressional representative to support your project earmarked in proposed legislation, you will need to "play the local card," as one experienced lobbyist told me, that is, you will need to show that representative how the proposed project earmarked for funding affects her district directly. Simply telling her that the project will be good for the state is not as convincing as showing how it will be good for the district. On the other hand, in grant negotiations with a bureaucrat in the Department of Education the "local card" is likely to be a lot less persuasive than it is with a congressional representative.

Political Appointees as Negotiators

Elected politicians appoint individuals to help carry out functions for which they are ultimately responsible. Thus governors and mayors appoint executive department heads to do the work of the executive, and legislators appoint legislative staff to help them in the task of making laws. These political appointees not only do their political masters' bidding, they can also influence their positions on many issues. Their ability to influence the politician who appointed them depends on the nature of their relationship with that politician. They are also keenly aware of how a potential decision in a negotiation may affect the political fortunes and the policies of the person who appointed them. As a result, as most lobbyists know, convincing a staff member of an issue is a way to convince the legislator for whom he or she works.

Treasury Secretary Brady was a political appointee of the U.S. President. At the same time, a person appointed to head a government department, like Secretary Brady, needs the support of that department and often becomes its defender in dealing with other government departments. As a result, political appointees need to satisfy their political masters to stay in their jobs but they also have to satisfy the bureaucracy in their departments if they are to do their jobs.

In many negotiations, the political appointee who heads a government department may not have the power that the department's senior bureaucrats have. For example, a political appointee in charge of U.S. Air Force procurement felt that he was treated as "summer help" by the second ranking official in that department, a long-serving, knowledgeable bureaucrat who had conducted many negotiations over the years. Both she and other bureaucrats on the staff knew that political appointees come and go with regularity but that the senior bureaucracy stayed in place, a fact that was not lost on other bureaucrats or the companies they were negotiating with.

Bureaucrats as Negotiators

When you negotiate with a government, nine times out of ten you are actually negotiating with a bureaucrat. A bureaucrat is a member of a bureaucracy, a professional corps of officials organized in a hierarchy and operating under a set of supposedly impersonal and uniform rules and procedures.

A bureaucracy may consist of thousands of civil servants working in an enormously complex system like the U.S. Department of Defense or just a few employees in the town clerk's office in Concord, Massachusetts. Despite the vast differences in size and complexity, the Defense Department and the Concord town clerk's office organizations share some fundamental characteristics: a hierarchical form of organization that allocates specific responsibilities to its members and a set of rules that the bureaucracy's members are to follow and apply in carrying out their assigned tasks and responsibilities

Even in cases when you negotiate with an elected official such as a mayor or governor, or a politically appointed executive such as a cabinet member or a state department head, neither of whom is technically part of a government bureaucracy, the bureaucracy is usually a powerful, though sometimes unseen presence at the bargaining table for at least two reasons. First, members of the bureaucracy will ordinarily have advised or informed political officials about the negotiation in which you are engaged. Indeed, the official with whom you are negotiating will usually depend on the bureaucracy's expertise in the subject matter and knowledge of the applicable rules in order to negotiate with you in any meaningful way. For example, no mayor will talk with you about your proposed shopping center without receiving the advice of the zoning department and the town engineer.

Second, wise officials know that despite their legal authority they risk serious organizational problems if they negotiate without seeking the bureaucracy's views or make agreements against the advice of the bureaucracy. For one thing, they will have to expend time, effort, and political capital to ensure that such agreements are implemented by the bureaucracy. For another, if they engage in this kind of free-wheeling behavior too often, they may find that they will have difficulty in leading the bureaucracy in other areas of their responsibility. While politicians come and go, as former President Gerald Ford recognized, "One of the enduring truths of the nation's capital is that bureaucrats survive."[6] Politicians and negotiators forget or ignore this maxim at their peril. Thus even though Buffett was negotiating with Brady directly over the phone, the Treasury bureaucracy was a powerful background presence. Brady was not likely to have overturned the ban if the Treasury bureaucracy had been vehemently opposed.

Deciding on Your Opening Move

Having found the right governmental units to negotiate with, you then have to decide how to begin negotiations. The old admonition that "you never get a second chance to make a first impression" underscores the importance of first impressions in interactions between persons. Just as first impressions in a job interview may mean the difference between being hired and being rejected, opening moves in a negotiation can influence the course of the discussion either positively or negatively for a long time afterward. Opening moves may even be the difference between making the deal and walking away empty-handed. As a result, you should carefully plan your opening moves in any negotiation.

Remember that opening moves not only communicate what you want, they may also communicate something about you and the organization you represent. Thus, your counterpart across the table may interpret your overly aggressive opening move as an indication that you and your organization are unreasonable, arbitrary, and perhaps untrustworthy. Once they have formed that impression, it may be difficult if not impossible to persuade them to change their evaluation, no matter how sweet and gentle you become in subsequent negotiating sessions.

You can begin to get an idea of the complexity of the challenges by considering the situation of the St. Lawrence Cement Company at the outset of its attempt to build a new cement plant in the Hudson Valley. It knew it had to obtain seventeen permits from a variety of local, state, and federal agencies. But where should it begin? Should it make applications for all seventeen permits all at once? In view of the emerging public interest in the project, it was likely that successfully obtaining one important permit would have an impact on how other agencies would view the project. An early success with one agency would encourage other agencies to act in the company's favor. An early failure would have just the opposite effect. As a result, the negotiation for each of the seventeen permits could not be seen as separate and distinct activities. They were interrelated. Thus, opening moves and subsequent sequencing of moves became very important for the St. Lawrence Cement Company, as they are for the successful negotiation of any major transaction with a government.

Care in developing opening moves in negotiations is particularly important in negotiations with governments. One of the most important moves you can make is deciding which government department to approach to start negotiations with. Beginning with the wrong office or the wrong person in that office sends messages to the entire bureaucracy, as we discussed earlier in this chapter.

The array of possible opening moves in a negotiation is often broader and more varied than one might assume at first glance. It is important to consider carefully the whole range of ways of starting a particular negotiation before deciding on the one to use.

The St. Lawrence Cement Company chose to focus its initial efforts on securing a permit from the New York State Department of Environmental Conservation (DEC) because it believed that the procedures and the standards followed by that department would be more favorable to the company than those applied in other New York State departments. The problem was that the law governing the permitting process in the DEC did not impose time limits on the agency As a result of the growing political controversy engendered by the plant, the DEC allowed the process to grind on without resolution for five years. In short, like many government agencies forced to handle a potentially damaging conflict, it opted for a strategy of delay.

After five years of effort with no decision, the St. Lawrence Cement Company decided to shift its efforts to securing a permit to the New York State Department of State (DOS) because although the DOS standards were somewhat tougher, it was required to make a decision within six months. The company declared that a permit from the DOS would be a "bellwether" for its negotiations with other agencies. After a review of six months, the DOS decided to deny the permit. Two weeks later, the St. Lawrence Cement Company formally announced that it was abandoning plans to build a new plant.[7] Had the company chosen to approach the DOS as its opening move, it would have saved the time and costs entailed in six years of fruitless negotiations.

Counterpart Access: Getting City Hall to Talk to You

Having decided whom you want to negotiate with and how you want to open discussions, your next task is to actually engage that person in negotiations. In order to do that, you need "access." The word "access" in the lexicon of experienced negotiators does not simply mean the ability to enter a government building or office. It means in particular the ability to engage in meaningful discussions with the specific government official who you believe has the power and the authority to give you what you want. You may through skillful analysis and investigation select just the right government official to talk to about your problem, but you have no assurance that person will be willing to talk to you. Remember, your right of petition guaranteed by the U.S. Constitution doesn't also require a government official to listen to you. Brady didn't have to take Buffett's telephone call. The fact that Brady did accept the call and was willing to talk about Salomon Brothers' problem meant that Buffett had access to Brady.

The Four Rs of Governmental Access

The challenge for negotiators with governments is therefore to gain access to the right counterpart who will help them achieve what they are seeking. What will give you access to that person so that you can begin negotiations? You need to have one of the four Rs of governmental access: a right, a relationship, a reputation, or resources.

Access by Right

For certain kinds of transactions, gaining access to an appropriate government representative to conduct your negotiation is not too difficult. For routine transactions, like obtaining a building permit in your town or registering a stock offering with the SEC, the government department or agency concerned has usually designated an official or office to deal with the public on such matters. Access in those situations is a matter of right, pursuant to some law or regulation. But *physical* access may not be enough to enable you to engage the government in a negotiation. You also need *intellectual* access. Even if a government department or agency has created an office or procedure to receive your request, it may nonetheless for internal political or bureaucratic reasons refuse to consider it in any meaningful way. Your request goes to the bottom of the pile and stays there. For example, when Maryland enacted legislation authorizing the creation of charter schools by local school boards, the Baltimore school system, which had opposed the new law, received charter school applications but the bureaucracy did not act on them. Seeing the charter schools as competing for funding with established public schools, the Baltimore school system let applications languish in bureaucratic limbo until it was forced to act on them by the courts.

If you are seeking to negotiate a transaction that is not routine, such as Buffett's request to change a Treasury decision or a "routine transaction" that presents special problems, like a charter school application in Baltimore, you need something more than a right of physical access. You need intellectual access, in the sense of being able to engage an appropriate government representative intellectually in order to be able to discuss your problem in a meaningful way. In those kinds of situations, you need something more than access by right.

Access by Relationship

An existing positive relationship with a government official or with someone, like a member of that person's staff, who has influence with that person is often an effective means of access. The fact that Brady knew and respected Buffett and therefore had a relationship with him allowed Buffett to gain access to Brady. While government officials try hard to give the appearance that they exercise their functions in an impersonal, objective manner, in practice they, like business executives, clergymen, athletes, or most anyone else for that matter, are influenced—at least with respect to access—by existing, positive relationships with other persons.

In situations where you do not have access to a particular government official or department, you might hire someone who does. For example, if you want to negotiate a grant from the U.S. Department of Housing and Urban Development (HUD), you might engage a law firm with experience in negotiating HUD transactions, not only for their knowledge of the relevant law and regulations but also for their relationships with key HUD officials. And if you are seeking to develop important business relations in a key country, you might engage a former U.S. ambassador to that country to help you gain access to decision makers through the ambassador's relationships with them.

Lobbyists' principal assets are the network of relationships that they have developed with senators, congressional representatives, their staff, and bureaucrats throughout government. It is these relationships that enable lobbyists to lobby. It is because of these relationships that they gain access to decision makers and therefore are able to advocate on behalf of the interests of their clients. Often lobbyists have gained those relationships through their own previous professional experience as politicians, congressional staffers, or bureaucrats themselves or because of the favors they have done for those persons in the past. Tommy Corcoran, the legendary Washington lobbyist, built valuable relations with officials throughout the government because during his long career he had helped them obtain government jobs, beginning when he was a member of President Franklin Roosevelt's White House inner circle during the New Deal era.[8] It is not only lobbyists who need relationships. Anyone who deals with governments needs them. As Jane Alexander, former head of the National Endowment for the Arts, reflected on her own government experience: "In Washington, you are only as valuable as the people who know you and support your cause, and so the modus operandi is to keep increasing your list of acquaintances."[9]

A relationship is a sense of connection between two or more persons that the persons involved believe bring them actual or potential benefits. Because of that relationship, one is disposed to allow another person to have access for purposes of communication, if for no other reason than not to damage that relationship and thereby put in jeopardy potential future benefits. A refusal by Brady to take Buffett's call or to discuss the ban on Salomon Brothers would certainly have had a negative impact on their relationship and that factor had to have contributed to Brady's decision to give Buffett access.

Relationships with government officials can be built in a number of ways, such as through working together, social interaction, favors done in the past, or mutual acquaintances. Relationships can also be gained through money, which is one of the reasons that corporate executives make financial contributions to politicians. These contributions help to give executives access to politicians and their staffs at some time in the future to discuss policies and legislation that may affect their business interests. For many years, Pfizer, the multinational drug company, had a policy of not contributing to the campaigns of politicians outside the United States. As its operations and interests became more global in scope, it found that it did not have the needed access to politicians and bureaucrats in other countries to discuss important policies affecting drug development and sales in those countries. It ultimately decided to begin making political campaign contributions abroad and as a result gained the access that it needed.

Access Through Reputation

Government officials and politicians, like anyone else, are influenced by the reputation of the person with whom they are negotiating. Even though they personally do not know an individual, they are usually more disposed to give access to a person they have heard of than someone who to them is an unknown. Thus the reputation of the negotiator or the company he or she represents may give that negotiator access to a politician or official that he might not otherwise have. Buffett's reputation as an immensely wealthy, shrewd, and successful investor and philanthropist gives him access to government departments and politicians that most of us would not have. If an official knows your reputation, he or she is more likely to take your phone call, accept a meeting, or genuinely listen to what you have to say than if they had never heard of you.

This is one of the reasons why well-known former politicians and officials join consulting firms, investment banks, law firms, and transnational corporations. Their reputations open government doors to those organizations that might otherwise remain closed. So famous politicians like former Senator and Republican presidential candidate Robert Dole and former U.S. Secretary of State Henry Kissinger have made lucrative second careers as negotiators with governments. Their key assets are not only their knowledge and relationships but also their reputations, which give them access to government leaders and officials to transact business on behalf of their clients. Think about it: If you were a government official or bureaucrat, would you refuse to take a call from Henry Kissinger or Bob Dole?

Related to the issue of access through reputation is the *title* of the person seeking access. Politicians, political appointees, and bureaucrats are intensely sensitive to status and prestige. They often see their own status and prestige as enhanced or diminished by the people they do business with. Thus it is often the case that they will grant access to the representative of an organization if they judge that person to be of a sufficiently high level, and they will refuse access to lesser beings. For example, if you are the Chairman and CEO of an oil company, you will probably gain access to the Minister of Petroleum of a Middle Eastern Company, but if you are a vice president you may wait forever for a meeting.

Access Through Resources

A fourth means of access arises from the resources that a negotiator commands. Companies like Wal-Mart or Toyota, seeking to make a major investment in a locality, usually have no trouble in gaining access to government officials and politicians to discuss their projects and their needs from the governments concerned. Indeed, the announcement that Toyota or Daimler-Chrysler is considering the construction of an auto plant in one of several possible American states usually results in a competition among those states, often led by governors, to attract those companies to a particular state to the exclusion of others. Neither Toyota nor

Daimler-Chrysler would have a problem of access to any government office in any of the states under consideration, simply because those government offices see those companies' resources as offering genuine benefits to their localities and therefore to their politicians and officials. Similarly, the ability of Warren Buffett to control vast resources is a powerful reason for most politicians and bureaucrats to give him access to their offices and to take his telephone calls.

Access Is Only the Beginning

Gaining access to the appropriate government official is only the beginning of the negotiation. Access by no means guarantees that you will get what you want. Having gained access, you must now set in motion a process that will result in a decision by the government negotiators on the other side of the table that will get you the agreement you are seeking. A decision on that agreement is usually not the official's alone to make. Just as Brady's decision was a decision of the U.S. Treasury and not of Nicholas Brady in his individual capacity, the decision that you as a negotiator are seeking is that of the government department or agency with which you are dealing, whether it's your town planning board, your state department of education, or the U.S. Department of Defense. The following chapters will provide guidance on structuring and guiding a negotiation process that will get you what you want.

Conclusion: Six Rules for Penetrating and Engaging Government Organizations

Follow these simple rules to handle the organizational dimensions of your government negotiations:

Rule #1: Research and analyze the way the government is organized. Try to learn how particular government departments actually behave. Make a map of critical governmental units and keep it up to date.

Rule #2: Identify all of the various government units that need to be involved in securing what you are seeking in the negotiation and learn the history of their relationships. Determine which units need to be at the negotiating table, which need to be parties to any agreement, and which need only to be kept informed.

Rule #3: Determine the right opening move to penetrate that organization and the proper sequence in approaching each unit to be followed thereafter.

Rule #4: Having identified the unit, next figure out the person or persons within that unit who can best help you.

Rule #5: Understand that government negotiators fall into one of three classes: politicians, political appointees, and bureaucrats. It is important to analyze how their particular interests and world views may affect the negotiation.

Rule #6: Determine the best means that will give you access to that person and particularly which of the four Rs of access—right, relationship, reputation, or resources—you should play on.

• CHAPTER FIVE •

The Political Imperative

The Special Nature of Government Interests and How They Affect Negotiations

> "The secret of negotiation is to harmonize the interests of the parties concerned."
>
> —FRANÇOIS DE CALLIÈRES (1716)

In the mid-1970s, a group of English and Hong Kong property developers signed a contract with the Egyptian government to build a "destination resort" near the famous Giza pyramids just outside of Cairo. As work began on the Pyramids project, public opposition rapidly grew both inside and outside of Egypt against what opponents called the construction of "a Disneyland" that would desecrate one of the world's great archeological treasures. Facing intense pressure both domestically and internationally, the Egyptian government cancelled the project.

In response, the investors, claiming a breach of contract, sued the Egyptian government in international arbitration for millions of dollars in damages. The government defended itself strenuously during the next fifteen years as the case made its way first through arbitration at the International Chamber of Commerce in Paris, then through the courts of France, and finally in arbitration at the

World Bank's International Centre for Settlement of Investment Disputes. Ultimately in 1993, an international tribunal awarded the investors $27.6 million, plus $5 million in costs, a decision that Egypt at first appealed before finally agreeing to settle with the investors for $17.5 million.

A Prime Minister's Calculation

In 1990, the Egyptian government and the investors, after lengthy negotiations, had tentatively agreed to settle the case for $10 million. To become final, the deal had to be approved by Egypt's prime minister. His aides strongly urged him to accept the settlement. They argued that the arbitration tribunal hearing the case would almost certainly rule against the government for substantially more, that the litigation was causing Egypt to expend large amounts of money and time to defend itself, and that the longstanding, festering dispute over the Pyramids project was negatively affecting the country's investment climate as other potential foreign investors viewed it as raising questions about the reliability of government commitments. For the government officials who had negotiated the settlement, the deal made sound economic sense.

As the prime minister weighed the arguments in favor of approving the settlement, he asked his aides what his other options were. They replied that the only other alternative was for Egypt to continue to defend itself in arbitration at great cost and to endure the negative reaction that the case engendered among other foreign investors. With only a moment's reflection, the prime minister concluded it would be preferable to continue the litigation. Approving the $10 million settlement, he said, "would not be in the country's best interests."

The prime minister's aides were mystified at this result, until a few month later in a relaxed conversation he explained privately to one of them that an agreement to settle the case for $10 million would have opened him to attack by political opponents and the media for having "sold out to foreigners," showing weakness in defending national interests, and possibly having taken a bribe. In an uncertain political position because of other factors, the prime minister decided not to run that risk. After all, the case had been going on for over a decade. A few more years of litigation could hardly matter.

The decision not to approve the settlement was, clearly, taken in the prime minister's interests, not the country's. The prime minister's overriding interests were political. Like many negotiators who represent governments, the prime minister was responding to the political imperatives of the situation. His principal interest was to maintain his position as prime minister, and he steadfastly refused to take any action, like paying a $10 million settlement to foreigners, that would put that position in jeopardy. As a result, the case continued for another three years, and Egypt finally settled for nearly twice the amount proposed in the original deal in 1990. By that time, someone else had become prime minister.

The response of the Egyptian prime minister was by no means unique. In the United States, government officials at all levels consider carefully the political implications of their decisions before making them. When faced with highly contentious issues, their basic strategy, like that of the prime minister, is to delay. So when various New York State departments perceived the full extent of the controversy surrounding the proposed construction of the new cement plant in the Hudson Valley, they delayed for six years until the regulations forced a decision.

It is interesting to speculate how a similar dispute between two private companies would have been resolved. Had the CEO of a corporation being sued for breach of contract been presented with a similar offer of settlement, that CEO would almost certainly have approved it since it would have been to the company's economic advantage to settle for less than the likely amount of a future judgment against it, to avoid continued legal costs and the expenditure of executive time, and to end litigation that might be adversely affecting other business relationships and opportunities. In short, a corporate CEO in a similar situation would have responded to the economic imperatives of the situation. This is not to say that CEOs in the private sector are not influenced by political considerations in their negotiations. The difference is that whereas *economic* imperatives tend to influence private sector negotiators predominantly, *political* imperatives tend to predominate in the thinking and the calculations of government negotiators.

The Importance of Interests

We have previously defined negotiation as a process of communication by which two or more parties seek to advance their own interests or those of the persons they represent through an agreement on a desired future action. At the heart of any negotiation is a desire by the parties to satisfy their interests. It is the very reason why the two sides are sitting across the table from one another.

If the secret of successful negotiation is to find a way to harmonize the interests of the parties, as François de Callières, an early, insightful negotiation commentator observed in his classic work *On the Manner of Negotiating with Princes*,[1] then it is crucial for each side to understand both its interests and those of the persons sitting across the table. You can't harmonize interests unless you first understand them.

The first rule of negotiation is therefore to understand interests, both your own and the other person's. This isn't as easy as it sounds. Although people negotiate to get what they want, they often fail or refuse to reveal what that is. Instead, they make demands and stake out positions and then try to impose them on the other person, an approach that often prevents agreement. The following true story illustrates the problem.

A wealthy man died and left all his property to be divided equally between his two daughters, Janet and Claire. All went smoothly until they came to the old man's ring, a diamond signet that he had worn most of his life. Both daughters wanted it, and each justified her position on a principle. Janet pointed to the fact that she had taken care of their father in his final illness. Claire claimed he had promised her the ring years before. Their positions seemed irreconcilable, and relations between the two sisters grew tense. Finally, in frustration, Janet asked Claire a key question: "*Why* do you want the ring?" Claire replied, "Because it has a beautiful diamond. I thought I'd make a pendant out of it." Janet responded, "I want it because it reminds me of Dad."

Once the two sisters realized that their underlying interests, though different, weren't necessarily mutually exclusive, they explored solutions to their common problem. They finally agreed that Claire would have the diamond replaced with Janet's birthstone, return the ring to Janet, and keep the diamond. This was an example of a win-win negotiation—one that allowed both sisters to satisfy their underlying interests.

Whether you are negotiating with your sister or your government, this story imparts some useful lessons about the importance of interests in negotiation and about ways of dealing with them:

1. *Uncover and discuss interests.* Like Janet and Claire, many negotiators state their positions forthrightly but don't reveal the interests and needs behind those positions. This can cause the other person to make false assumptions—and to see the process as a battle of wills. The task of uncovering interests is particularly difficult in negotiations with government officials for they, like the Egyptian prime minister, are generally reluctant to admit that their primary interest in the negotiation is the political imperative of holding on to their jobs

2. *Ask the right questions.* If the other person doesn't reveal why she wants what she wants, probe deeper by asking questions that begin with the word "why." If this doesn't work, speculate. To deal with a reticent Claire, Janet might have said, "I guess you want the ring to sell for cash." That might have provoked Claire to correct her by saying, "No, I want the ring because I like the diamond." Had the negotiators for the investors in the Pyramids case been wiser they might have appreciated the political difficulties that a settlement would pose for the prime minister and therefore would have raised that issue with their counterparts in an effort to find a way of structuring a settlement so as to minimize negative public reaction to the deal.

3. *Reveal your own interests.* Problem-solving negotiation is a *mutual* process. An effective way to encourage the other person to talk about his or her interests is to talk about your own.

4. *Make your negotiations problem-solving exercises.* A negotiation is most productive when both people see it as a way to solve a common problem, rather then a contest of wills or a debate over positions.

5. *Create options together.* Once interests are out in the open, suggest options that will satisfy those interests. Unlike a position that can be satisfied only by its acceptance, an interest can often be advanced in several different ways. Thus, if the negotiators in the Egyptian case had recognized and discussed in an open way the political implications of a settlement, they might have developed some creative options to deal with the prime minister's potential political problem.

The Many Faces of Interests

In most negotiations, several different interests are at work on each side of the negotiating table. For example, the Egyptian government negotiators who arrived at a settlement with the investors were pursing at least three distinct but related interests:

1. To reduce the liability of Egypt to the investors
2. To eliminate further costs related to the law suit
3. To improve the investment climate of their country in the eyes of potential investors

But in addition to the interests above, in any negotiation, as we saw with the prime minister, there are always the personal interests of the negotiators. At the bargaining table, you are not negotiating with the government as an entity. You are negotiating with a human agent of the government—a politician, a political appointee, or a bureaucrat. That agent is seeking to advance the interests of the government, but also, like the Egyptian prime minister, that agent has personal interests to defend as well. Those interests are usually political and relate very much to maintaining or enhancing that agent's political position or that of the unit to which he or she is attached. As a result, in a negotiation with any government, to truly understand the interests at work on the other side of the table, you need to understand the officially stated interests of the government, whether it is achieving an effective land use plan for a community or creating an attractive investment climate for a country, but you also need to understand the professional and personal interests of the official with whom you are negotiating. As in the case of the Egyptian prime minister, those interests are usually not stated but they nonetheless can have a powerful effect on the course of the negotiation. Thus an important rule to follow in negotiating with a government politician or government official is: *Always search for the political imperative driving that politician or official.*

Finding the Political Imperative in a Government Negotiation

Identifying the political imperatives driving the negotiators on the other side of the table is difficult because government negotiators, like the Egyptian prime minister, rarely will admit them, let alone discuss them at length. Both in the negotiating room and outside, government negotiators invariably explain their actions in altruistic terms as advancing the national interest, protecting public welfare, or defending the community. They will almost never admit that their negotiating positions and strategies are motivated by a desire to protect their positions, advance their careers, or defend their department's budget and autonomy. In short, they will hardly ever admit that the political imperative has any influence at all on their actions. To do so would open them to charges that they are not carrying out their fundamental mission as government officials, which is to do the government's business not their own, thereby weakening themselves at the negotiating table and reducing their influence within government.

The nature and intensity of the political imperative will vary from negotiation to negotiation. The political imperative may also be driven by other particular concerns, which in many cases are defensive in nature. They represent a desire by an official, like the Egyptian prime minister, to defend an advantageous position.

Among the most common political interests pursued by government negotiators are:

1. ***Defending Against Political Opponents.*** In the Egyptian prime minister's case, the political imperative to which he was responding was the desire to protect himself from attacks by opponents and thereby increase the likelihood that he would retain his political position. To understand whether this interest is at work in your negotiation, you should consider to what extent the agreements you are asking for will open the government negotiators on the other side of the table to attacks from their bureaucratic or political adversaries, both inside and outside of government. If you conclude that such attacks are likely, you need to develop a strategy that will limit or blunt their effect on the government officials with whom you are negotiating.

2. ***Defending the Interests of Constituents.*** All government departments have constituents on whom they depend and therefore they may take action in negotiations to protect those constituents' interests or prevent their constituents from acting against the government official in question. Thus, as we discussed in Chapter 2, the Japanese government in its negotiation with Raytheon over building a weapons system was careful not to choose between the two politically powerful electronics companies whose support the government valued. On the other hand, the European governments moved to protect their important constituent weapons companies by directing Raytheon to negotiate with those companies, not with the companies that Raytheon had chosen on its own.

3. ***Defending Resources.*** All government departments require resources—money, people, and equipment—in order to function and to maintain their authority. The need to protect those resources is a powerful imperative in negotiations. Thus, fearing that charter schools would draw resources from traditional public schools, the Baltimore school system, in classic passive-aggressive fashion, simply refused to consider applications for charter schools until a court ordered it to do so.

4. ***Defending Autonomy and Authority.*** More than resources, government departments and agencies value authority and auton-

omy, and they usually furiously resist actions that lead to the loss of these two vital commodities of governance. In any negotiation you should ask how the result you are seeking may affect the autonomy and authority of the officials with whom you are negotiating. For example, any transaction that will require two or more government agencies or departments to cooperate may be presented as being in the public interest but will be seen by the departments concerned as threatening their autonomy and authority and therefore definitely not in their bureaucratic interests.

5. *Defending Career Interests.* A constant question in the minds of any government negotiator is: How will this negotiation affect my career? Bureaucrats are concerned about "career-enhancing activities" and "career-destroying activities." They eagerly seek the former and assiduously try to avoid the latter. The question weighs more heavily on some officials than on others, but it is always there. For example, in one negotiation over mineral rights in a Middle Eastern developing country, the representative of the American company and the deputy minister of mineral resources developed a strong, friendly relationship but the negotiations seemed to be going nowhere. After dinner one evening, the American executive asked what the problem was, and the deputy minister replied: "I have to be frank with you. If I make a deal with your competitor who is well known to the government ministers, the deal will be approved with no problems. If I make a deal with your company that has never operated in our country before, any deal that I make will be questioned. Even though your company will probably do a better job for us because your technology is more effective, I just can't take the chance. I have two years to go before retirement and I need to protect my position in government and my pension. Also, my wife and son both work for the government, so I can't do anything that will put them in danger, either." Then he added, "But if it will help you with your company, we can continue to negotiate, if you want to."

One defensive strategy that officials often use to defend their career interests is to follow the rules assiduously. The rules, which have usually been set down by some higher authority, function to protect that official from career-damaging criticism and censure. If you are seeking to achieve an innovative transaction in your negotiation that is not specifically authorized by the rule, you are likely to encounter an old bureaucratic maxim: "Never do anything for the first time." You will therefore need to find a tactic to blunt bureaucratic aversion to innovation.

The Intensity of the Political Imperative

The strength of the political imperative will vary from negotiation to negotiation. As a general rule, its importance in a particular negotiation is inversely related to the sense of security that the government negotiator feels. Thus a government negotiator who is strongly secure in his position tends to be less influenced by the political imperatives of the situation than one who is less secure. The Egyptian prime minister's decision to refuse the settlement was clearly influenced by his political sense of insecurity. A politically powerful leader with strong public support, for example, the late President Nasser, would have been less concerned about attacks from political opponents and therefore more willing to approve the deal.

In a similar vein, it has been noted that many European regulators appear to be more flexible and accommodating with the companies they regulate than are comparable U.S. regulators. One explanation for this difference is that European regulators have a more secure base of authority within their governments than do American regulators.[2] The more insecure the regulator, the more that regulator will take inflexible positions and operate strictly according to the rules in order to ward off criticism and attacks from opponents and the general public. Politically secure regulators, on the other hand, can take innovative, flexible positions because they feel less threatened by potential opponents and the public. Thus, as part of your preparation for negotiation, you should determine the political bases of support of the agency with which you are negotiating as well as of the individual who sits on the other side of the table.

Coping with the Political Imperative

If you sense that the political imperative is strongly at work in your negotiation, you need to develop strategies and tactics that will allow both you and your counterpart to deal with it. Generally, use the approach recommended by François de Callières: find a means to harmonize the political interests of the government negotiators with your own interests in doing the deal. Here are a few coping strategies:

Strategy #1: Involve Third Parties in the Negotiation or in the Deal

One way to deal with the political imperative in certain negotiations is to involve a third party in the negotiation or in the deal itself. The presence of an appropriate third party either to endorse the negotiation or to participate in the transaction has the effect of reducing the demands of the political imperative and thereby limiting its influence on the decision-making process of the negotiators on the other side of the table. A third party serves to deflect the political heat from opponents that may be caused by what you are seeking to achieve in the negotiation.

For this tactic to work, you have to choose an appropriate third party. Any third party will not do. An appropriate third party in general is a person or persons who have a status within the society that can change and hopefully reduce the political imperatives influencing the government negotiators on the other side of the table. For example, in the case of Egypt's proposed settlement over the failed destination resort project, the prime minister might have appointed a panel of distinguished persons to review the proposed settlement and give its opinion on whether it was fair to Egypt. Had the negotiators for the investors been more sensitive to Egyptian political realities, they themselves might have suggested the idea to their Egyptian counterparts at the time they agreed on the terms of settlement. A favorable recommendation by such a panel would have given some protection to the Egyptian prime minister from political opponents and the media.

A similar technique was used in India in the mid-1990s in a dispute between the Dabhol Power Company, created by a group of American investors that included Enron, General Electric, and Bechtel, and the State of Maharashtra, one of the country's most economically important states. Prior to constructing the largest power plant in India, the State of Maharashtra, then controlled by the Congress Party, had signed a thirty-year contract with the Dabhol Power Company to purchase all the electricity that the plant would produce. As the plant was under construction, an election campaign took place in Maharashtra in which the opposition BJP–Shiv Sena party challenged the legality, propriety, and economic soundness of the contract. The contract became the major issue in the election. When the BJB–Shiv Sena won the election and took control of the government, it cancelled the electricity supply contract with Dabhol, declaring, "We shall not renegotiate."

Within a short time, Dabhol showed a willingness to offer the state more favorable terms and the government, facing a $300 million law suit and the need to solve the power shortage facing the state, sought a way out of the impasse. The political imperatives caused by the political campaign, the abrupt cancellation, and the governing party's hostile rhetoric against the Dabhol Power Company made direct, face-to-face negotiations between the government and the power company impossible. To resolve the impasse, the government appointed a "panel of industry experts" to renegotiate the power purchase agreement with the Dabhol Power Company and to make recommendations on a new contract to the government. Thus, in a formal sense, the government was not dealing with its former nemesis the Dabhol Power Company, but with a group of Indian experts who could be expected to defend the national interest.[3]

One of the reasons that the Dabhol Power project ran into trouble was the failure of the American negotiators to consider the political imperatives affecting the transaction. The project was the biggest foreign investment in a country that was acutely sensitive to foreign investment, especially in a sector that had historically been dominated by government provision of electricity. Bechtel, which had decades of experience building projects throughout the world, urged Enron, the lead investor in the project, to take a local Indian partner into the deal. Enron, showing the arrogance that would later lead to its downfall, said that a foreign partner was not necessary and that Enron was totally capable of developing and executing the power project on its own. Clearly, the purpose of a local partner was not to provide advanced technology but to handle the political imperatives created by the deal. With an Indian partner, the project would have been less vulnerable to charges by Indian politicians that foreigners were exploiting the country.

The involvement of an appropriate third party is a useful tactic in blunting the demands of the political imperative in dealing with all levels of government, not only abroad but in the United States as well. For example, suppose that a chemical company wants the state environmental regulator to approve the use of a new, cleaner, and more environmentally friendly waste treatment technology that is not completely covered by published regulations. The environmental agency is naturally reluctant to approve since it will be blamed for any performance failure. To deal with this reluctance, the company might propose a trial use of the technology with respected environmental organizations overseeing and evaluating the new technology's performance. Such a process might reduce the political imperative felt by the state environmental agency.[4]

Strategy #2: Find Other Resources (preferably someone else's)

If what you are seeking from a government department or agency will have a negative impact on its budget or resources, you can expect strong resistance from that department or agency. One technique to deal with the resistance of this political imperative is to find substitute resources for the department or agency concerned. Sometimes you may have to provide the resources yourself. For example, if you are seeking to obtain a permit to hold a public event and the city is unwilling to give it to you because its budget can't support the additional police protection needed, you may have to provide the money for overtime police if you want that permit.

Sometimes, you can find help to obtain those resources from a third party. Indeed, the ideal solution to the problem is to persuade a third party to provide the resources that the government needs so that you can get what you want. For example, for many years the Chicago offices of the U.S. Department of the Treasury were located in a building owned by Joseph P. Kennedy, the father of the then-future President. The elder Kennedy wanted the Treasury to move out so he could use the space for more profitable purposes, but he knew that trying to evict Treasury would be a futile and politically damaging enterprise. With the Treasury's consent, he instead engaged Tommy Corcoran, the powerful Washington lobbyist, to persuade Congress to pass a law authorizing the U.S. Treasury to construct its own building in Chicago.[5] This tactic allowed Kennedy to harmonize his interests in regaining control over his building with the Treasury's interests in having sufficient space to meet its operational needs, while at the same time elevating its status, prestige, and visibility in the city.

Strategy #3: Give Credit Even Where It May Not Be Due; Accept Blame Even Where It May Not Be Yours

Just as stock options and bonuses are the currencies of corporate executive existence, credit and blame are the currency of government life. It is credit for good things that enhances careers and political positions. It is blame for bad things that destroys political and bureaucratic careers and undermines political positions. Politicians, political appointees, and bureaucrats therefore eagerly seek recognition from their superiors and the public for accomplishments that are deemed worthwhile and equally vigorously try to avoid responsibility for actions that are considered detrimental to the government or the public. It is important to remember that in every negotiation you undertake with a government official at any level that official is always calculating whether the negotiation will generate career-enhancing credit or career-crippling blame. This calculation is particularly salient in government transactions that are seen by the public, political adversaries, and government superiors as different or unusual.

Given the importance of the currency of credit and blame in

government life, you should consider how to use it effectively in your own negotiations with governments. In particular, how can you structure the negotiations and the ultimate transaction in a way that will reflect favorably on the government negotiators? To the extent that they envisage the deal will bring credit to them, they will be disposed to see it happen. Conversely, to the extent that they fear the deal will generate blame, they will work to oppose it. For example, if you are negotiating to obtain government approval to build a large project like a shopping mall, an aluminum smelter, or a cement plant, you might seek to include in the project elements like a playground, clinic, or social center and give credit to key local politicians for obtaining these community benefits by naming these facilities after them or allowing officials to conduct the ceremonies that open them. Make it known, however subtly, that in your public relations you will be lauding the government's contributions to the transaction.

You should also be willing to accept blame and express regret. As one experienced government affairs specialist told me, "I spend a lot of my time apologizing." For many business executives the idea of apologizing for their or their companies' actions is an anathema. John Gutfreund, the chairman and CEO of Salomon Brothers during the Treasury auction scandal, later remarked. "No apologies to anyone for anything. Apologies are bull_____."[6] That approach is a disastrous tactic in negotiations with a government. In fact, as a general rule when you or your organization has done something to offend a government official, whether it is a state trooper or the SEC, the best opening move is an apology.

Charles Prince, the Chairman of Citigroup, realized this when he began negotiations with the Japanese authorities after Citigroup's private banking operations in Japan had been caught violating the law. In 2004, the Japanese financial authorities discovered that Citigroup's private bank in Japan had engaged in several improper and illegal transactions over a period of time. It therefore took the draconian step of closing all Citigroup's private banking operations in the country, a step that would reduce the revenues of the world's largest bank by $100 million a year. Coming on the heels of other scandals in Citigroup's far-flung operations, the closure of its private banking business in Japan was a particularly harsh blow that needed a serious response by the bank's leadership.

To deal with the situation, Prince, who had been appointed CEO the previous year and had taken on the task of trying to change the bank's culture, fired three of the bank's top executives in New York, as well as several employees in Japan. He then flew to Tokyo to meet with Japanese authorities, apologize for Citigroup's behavior, and explain the steps it would take to clean up its act. At a large press conference, he took responsibility for Citigroup's actions, apologized for the bank's behavior, and then in a traditional Japanese act of contrition, bowed deeply from the waist, eyes fixed on the ground. News photographers captured this unique moment of Prince's bow of contrition, and it appeared on television and in the press around the world. As the *New York Times* commented: "It was a bow seen round the world, an unusually public *mea culpa* by the top executive of a financial giant that has typically circled its wagons when criticized or preferred closed door resolutions of problems."[7]

Strategy #4: Shift the Matter to a Friendlier Department

A government is not a monolith. Some governmental departments may be friendlier or at least more open to your request than others. Sometimes, it is possible to shift your efforts to another department—although it would have been better to have made the right choice at the beginning. This strategy is fraught with danger, however, since the less friendly department may resist it strongly and then, if you succeed, make life difficult for you and your organization thereafter.

Conclusion: Six Rules for Dealing with Interests in Government Negotiations

In view of the importance of dealing effectively with interests in any government negotiation, here are a few rules to follow in carrying out that crucial task.

Rule #1: Always look beyond the stated positions of the government and its negotiators. Try to understand the political interests that they are seeking to satisfy in your negotiation and the political imperatives to which they are responding.

Rule #2: Recognize that many interests may be in play on the other side of the table, including the personal and professional interests of the individual negotiators.

Rule #3: In seeking to understand the professional and personal interests of government negotiators, always search for the political imperatives influencing their decisions. The political imperatives to which government negotiators respond are usually to defend themselves against political opponents, to retain the support of vital constituents, and to preserve their resources, autonomy, authority, and career prospects.

Rule #4: Generally speaking, the power of political imperatives in a given negotiation will vary inversely to the sense of security that negotiators feel in their governmental position. Politically insecure officials are usually more influenced by political imperatives than are politically secure officials.

Rule #5: Techniques for dealing with the political imperative in a negotiation with government officials include the involvement of appropriate third parties, the inclusion of additional resources, giving credit to government negotiators, and protecting them from blame.

Rule #6: Don't be reluctant to apologize when necessary.

❖ ❖ ❖ ❖ ❖ ❖

We began this chapter with an observation from de Callières on the importance of harmonizing interests. Let's end it with another of his insights: "The great secret of negotiation is to bring out prominently the common advantage to both parties of any proposal and so to link those advantages that they may appear equally balanced to both parties."[8]

· CHAPTER SIX ·

Power Tools for Influencing Government Decisions

> Let no man imagine that he has no influence. Whoever he may be, and wherever he may be placed, the man who thinks becomes a light and a power.
>
> —HENRY GEORGE

When an individual faces a government in a negotiation, it seems that the government has all the power and that the individual has very little. As we have discussed earlier, governments normally have enormous forces at their command and are not timid in using them to defend their interests. Does this fact mean that an individual or company on the other side of the table is totally helpless in the face of government power? Are there no sources of power that individuals or companies can mobilize to use for their benefit?

To answer these questions, we first have to consider the nature of power.

The Nature of Negotiating Power

What is power, anyway? In particular, what is negotiating power?

In essence, power is the means by which a state, company, or individual attains a desired end in its relations with other states, companies, or individuals. Many people think that power refers to the physical resources that a company, country, or individual has at its command. In a negotiation between the U.S. Federal Government and a small, bankrupt auto dealership in Fargo, North Dakota, over unpaid income taxes, the federal government is powerful because of the vast resources, a huge organization, and numerous legal tools at its command. However, this emphasis on physical resources distorts the nature and role of power in a negotiation.

The goal of a negotiator in any negotiation is to convince the other side to agree to an action that is in the negotiator's interest. From this perspective, negotiating power means *the ability to influence or move the decisions of the other side at the bargaining table in a desired way.* In some situations, a party's physical resources, such as its capital, technology, or organization, may indeed influence the other side's decision. But in other cases, less tangible factors, such as an original idea, a strong relationship, or a reputation for honesty, may also be sources of influence and therefore of power at the negotiating table. These nonmaterial factors are important power tools for any negotiator. With some adaptation, they can be as effective with governments as with individuals. The following story, based on my own experience in negotiating a country agreement on behalf of the Ford Foundation with the Sudanese Ministry of Foreign Affairs, illustrates the use of important power tools in a government negotiation.

Convincing a Diplomat

The official with whom I was negotiating the country agreement was a bright and polished diplomat who had graduated from the University of Khartoum Law School, with which the Ford Foundation had a long association. He was extremely cordial and seemed eager that the Foundation expand its activities in the country since he felt that its assistance would be useful in many respects. As a result, our discussions went smoothly as we discussed the various issues to be included in the country agreement. However, when we reached the topic of tax and customs duties exemptions for the Foundation and its personnel, the agreeable smile on his face was replaced with a look of consternation.

Tax and customs exemptions for a purely private organization? The Foreign Ministry had never done that before. The Sudanese diplomat wasn't sure whether the ministry even had the power to grant such an exemption. Even if it did, he didn't know whether the government would be prepared to grant those exemptions to a wealthy foreign organization. Clearly, there were no definite rules on this topic, and that presented a problem to my counterpart and, by extension, to his superiors in the ministry. At that point in our conversations, it looked as if Sudan was not going to grant a tax exemption to the Ford Foundation. If that happened, I was fairly sure the Foundation would drop the whole idea of establishing an office in Sudan.

Like any other person negotiating with a government, I needed to find a way to influence a government official's decision in my favor. As we struggled over the issue, I tried to explain to the Sudanese diplomat that what I was asking for was really not that unusual and that in all the countries in which the Ford Foundation had offices the local government had granted it an exemption from taxes and customs duties. He nodded in understanding, but hardly seemed convinced. I then said that the Foundation had had such a country agreement for many years with Egypt, which was at that time the regional office for Foundation activities throughout the Middle East, including Ford programs in Sudan. If the Foundation didn't establish an office in Khartoum, it would be forced to operate its Sudanese programs from Cairo. Suddenly, the Sudanese diplomat brightened. "I would like to see the Egypt country agreement," he said. "Do you think you can get me a copy?" I replied that I would try.

The next day, before I was able to get through to our Cairo office using Sudan's uncertain international telecommunications system, I received a telephone call from the Ford Foundation's Regional Representative in Cairo. "What are you stirring up down there?" he asked. "Two people from the Sudanese embassy here just showed up unannounced at the office and asked to see a copy of our country agreement with Egypt. Should I give it to them?" With my encouragement, he sent a copy of the Foundation's Egyptian country agreement to the Sudanese embassy in Cairo, which then forwarded it by diplomatic pouch to the Foreign Ministry in Khartoum. The following week, the Sudanese diplomat and I agreed on a complete text of a country agreement between the Ford Foundation and the government of the Sudan. Its provisions on tax and customs exemptions followed the text of the Egyptian country agreement word for word.

The Power of Precedent

Finding an acceptable precedent was what allowed the Sudanese diplomat and me to reach agreement on exemptions to taxes and customs duties. An acceptable precedent influenced the diplomat to make a decision in my favor and was in effect an important power tool in my negotiation with the Sudanese government. A precedent is an act or example from the past that may be used to justify or guide action in similar cases in the future. All of us are influenced by past examples. When faced with a new situation that calls for a decision, we instinctively ask how we or others have dealt with similar situations in the past. That reaction is based on a belief that knowledge gained from the past can help us decide on a course of action for a future that we cannot possibly know.

To understand the perceptions and interests of your counterparts on the other side of the table, you have to put yourself in their position. As François de Callières insightfully wrote nearly three hundred years ago about the effective negotiator, "The more often [a negotiator] thus puts himself in the position of others, the more subtle and effective will his arguments be."[1] So put yourself in the position of the Sudanese diplomat sitting across the table from me. What were his interests? What was his problem?

The diplomat and his colleagues in the Foreign Ministry faced the problem of an uncertain future if they granted my request for a tax and customs duty exemption. Was granting a tax and customs duty exemption to the Ford Foundation and its personnel the right thing to do? No law or regulation specifically authorized that kind of special treatment for a purely private organization. If the government did give such an exemption, could it lead to bad results for the country, for the ministry, and—most important of all—for the officials who permitted it? Could the exemption be abused by this foreign foundation? Why should the Sudanese government treat the Ford Foundation any differently from other private organizations? After all, foreign corporations doing business in the country had to pay taxes and duties. Could the exemption be used by the Foundation to evade legitimate taxes that everybody else had to pay?

On the other hand, if the Sudanese government denied the exemption, would the Foundation provide less assistance to the country if it decided not to set up an office and instead continue to operate from Cairo? Would a Foundation presence in Khartoum mean that Sudan would receive more aid? Even if the diplomats with whom I was negotiating thought it would be a good idea to grant the exemption, how were they going to convince their superiors to go along? And what about the Ministry of Finance? Would it sit quietly by while tax revenue escaped capture by the public treasury?

These were some of the questions that were going through the mind of my counterpart as he sat across the table from me. In the absence of a specific rule, he needed some guidance both for himself and his superiors, guidance that gave some assurance that the grant of a tax and customs exemption would not prove to be a costly decision for his country and for his career.

It was the discovery of the precedent of the Foundation's Egyptian country agreement that put these questions to rest. If Egypt, Sudan's northern neighbor that had exerted significant political and economic influence in the Sudan for many years—indeed centuries—could grant a tax exemption to a private foundation with no apparent negative results, why couldn't Sudan do the same thing? After all, Egypt was just as concerned with protecting its national interests as was Sudan. Not only did the Egyptian experience reassure the Sudanese diplomat that he was doing the right thing, but it also gave him a power tool to persuade the foreign minister himself to approve and sign the agreement that we had negotiated. In addition, it gave the Foreign Ministry a means to defend its action with other Sudanese government departments that might want to challenge it. So finding the right precedent was the key to achieving a successful negotiation in the Sudan.

My experience in the Sudan was by no means unique. In any negotiation with a government, finding and applying the right precedent is the key to getting what you want. Precedent is a powerful means of influencing the decisions of government negotiators. Government negotiators, whether they are politicians, political appointees, or bureaucrats, need to demonstrate that they are treating people fairly. Allegations and, even worse, evidence of favoritism or bias by a government official toward particular individuals or groups are potentially career-damaging events. It is for this reason that following the rules is so important for government officials because its gives them protection from these kinds of allegations.

When no specific rules cover a situation, an established precedent is the next best kind of protection. What a precedent allows a government negotiators to do is to show that they are treating a current problem as has been done to similar problems in the past. They are treating like cases alike—one of the basic applications of our notions of fairness. It allows a government negotiator to demonstrate that his or her decision is not based on personal favoritism or prejudice but rather on principle—the principle demonstrated by the precedent. To act without a rule or an appropriate precedent places a government official in danger of attack by opponents and superiors.

The existence of a precedent in support of proposed government action, on the other hand, often provides a government official with desired protection from political opponents, superiors, the media, and the general public. Had the Egyptian prime minister, discussed in Chapter 5, been able to point to precedent of other prime ministers entering into settlements with other foreign investors, he might have been more willing to approve the settlement reached in the Pyramids hotel case. A precedent—or preferably several precedents—would have allowed him to defend himself against charges that he was weak, that he had sold out to foreigners, or that he had accepted a bribe. The lesson then is clear: In any negotiation with a government, always search for an appropriate precedent to justify your proposals and requests.

Precedent and Standards

In any negotiation, governmental or non-governmental, it is important for negotiators to use standards and objective criteria in justifying their demands and to ask their counterparts across the table to do the same. So if you are negotiating to buy a business, you are more effective in persuading the other side on the price if you base your offer on a discounted cash flow analysis of the business or the sales price of similar businesses in the area in the last year than simply to justify your offer on what you want to pay or how much you can afford. The use of standards in a negotiation has three advantages. First, it makes you more persuasive. Basing your request for a tax exemption on the fact that you have received a similar exemption in another country is more convincing than simply saying that a tax exemption would be nice to have. Second, the use of a standard or precedent avoids an emotional and usually damaging contest of wills and puts the discussion on a rational basis. And third, it provides a means for the person with whom you are negotiating to persuade his superiors or principals that the negotiated deal is one they should accept as being in the best interests of their organization.

A precedent is only one kind of standard. In your negotiations with governments, you may have a variety of standards to choose from in order to influence the decisions of government negotiators in your favor: market rate, recent sales, comparable property valuations, or the "going rate" for a particular good or service. Generally speaking the most persuasive standard in dealing with a government—particularly a government regulator—is the precedent of similar action by that department or regulator in the past in a similar case. If you want to build a motorcycle track in your backyard and you can show that the town planning board permitted one of your neighbors to build a motorcycle track two years ago, you have a powerful tool for persuading that town board to decide in your favor. Its persuasive force stems from the political imperative to which all government officials respond. For the town planning board not to decide in your favor would open it to charges of favoritism, prejudice, and the irrationality of not treating like cases alike. The failure to treat all citizens equally not only opens the town planning board to political attack, it also makes its decision vulnerable to challenge in the courts.

While historical precedent is a powerful influence in government negotiations, it is much less so in negotiations between private parties. For example, in buying a business, the historical precedent of what the same business sold for five years ago would have relatively little impact on the discussions. The consequent issue of treating like cases alike and all citizens equally is not really a consideration in private commercial negotiations because these negotiators are driven by the market imperative of achieving maximum gain rather than the political imperative of retaining or maximizing political power.

Finding the Right Precedent

In view of the power of precedent in government negotiations, it is important to find the right precedent as part of your preparation to negotiate with a government. A first step in finding the right precedent is, as we did in the case of the Sudanese diplomat, to put yourself in the position of the government officials with whom you are negotiating and to look at the issues under discussion from their point of view. Go through the kind of analysis we did earlier, identifying the questions that are most probably in the minds of your counterparts and then think about the precedent or standard that will answer those questions. Remember, in a real sense, every negotiated agreement is a prediction about the future, a prediction about benefits and costs. My goal in negotiating a tax exemption with Sudan was to convince the Sudanese that the exemption would yield maximum benefits at little cost. One way of assuring them that my prediction was justified was to show them what had happened in a similar case, the country agreement with Egypt.

In many negotiations you may have several historical precedents to choose from. In making your choice among possible options, you should be guided by two important criteria: specificity and relevance. The more *specific* you can be about the details of the precedent the more persuasive you are likely to be in convincing government officials or regulators that the precedent ought to govern their actions in their negotiation with you. For example, my statement to the Sudanese diplomat that the Ford Foundation had tax exemption agreements with many countries was less effective than my reference to the specific case of Egypt. Specific cases and concrete facts have a way of seizing the attention of other people more effectively than do generalities. More important, a specific case seems to afford greater assurance that the deal will happen as predicted than a bland general principle.

Second, the specific case or cases that you choose as precedent need to be *relevant* to the issues under negotiation. Thus for the Sudanese diplomat, the example of the Egyptian country agreement was probably the most persuasively relevant precedent I could have given because of Egypt's long and close relationship with the Sudan and its similarity in culture and political outlook. To have cited the country agreement with Indonesia or Brazil, although helpful, would have been much less convincing. Finding a precedent that is exactly like the case you are negotiating is often difficult and sometimes impossible. In those situations, your task as a negotiator is to show how a past case, that is apparently different from the one under negotiation, is actually relevant. So if you are negotiating with the town planning board to get permission to build that motorcycle track on your property, something that the town had never allowed before, you will want to identify other cases in which the town allowed exceptional construction on residential property—for example, an equestrian ring or a special garage for a collection of classic cars—and show how in effect those actions are the functional equivalent of what you are asking for. Isn't a track for horses similar to a track for motorcycles? Isn't allowing the owner to pursue his hobby of collecting classic cars on property really not much different from permitting an owner to pursue his passion for motorcycles? If the regulator has never specifically approved a project like yours, find examples of previously approved projects that have elements similar to yours.

Finding an appropriate precedent for your negotiation can be more difficult than locating the applicable law, regulation, or rule. Laws, regulations, and rules are usually published in accessible form. Precedents often are not. Appropriate precedents are stored in dusty filing cabinets and in people's memories. Sometimes they are reported in the press and sometimes not.

One means of uncovering these precedents is to talk to people in the government offices with which you will be negotiating. Before you actually present your proposal or sit down to negotiate with high-ranking officials, you are well advised to visit the government offices concerned and talk to low-level employees to gather information on the application process. In many cases, the employees at the operational level have had a long tenure in that office and therefore are a valuable source of memories about previous cases. Indeed, their knowledge of precedent may be much greater and more detailed than the knowledge of their superiors running that office. So the town clerk who has been around for twenty years may be a better source of precedent than the town manager who was hired last year and will probably move on to a new job in a few more.

A second important source of precedent is consultants, lawyers, and lobbyists whose main occupation in life is to help you in your negotiations with governments. Indeed, their basic capital is their knowledge of how a particular government office operates, what it has done or refused to do in the past, and who the people are who make that office function. As a result, it is rare for significant negotiations with a government not to include some type of consultant, lawyer, or lobbyist as part of the negotiating team.

The Power of Written Materials

The right written materials can also be effective in persuading the other side in a negotiation. One of the most important is a proposed draft of the agreement you want.

Draft Agreements

An important power tool at work in my negotiation with the Sudanese government was a draft. A draft is a written proposal of the agreement or approval that you are seeking to obtain from the government with which you are negotiating.

Several years ago, while teaching a negotiation training program, I kept asking participating African officials, "What's the toughest deal you've ever negotiated?" Their answer was fairly consistent: "The Boeing contract." At a time when their governments were seeking to develop state-run airlines and Boeing jets offered the best option to meet their needs, these officials, upon sitting down to negotiate the purchase with Boeing representatives, were immediately confronted with the manufacturer's several hundred–page, highly technical standard form contract that threw most of the risks of the deal on the buyer. To hear the officials tell the story, Boeing's attitude in the negotiation was "If you want the planes, sign the contract." While the Boeing example may be a bit extreme, the use of standard form agreements in negotiating all kinds of deals is—well—fairly standard.

Most people think that a negotiation goes through a fixed sequence of phases in which the parties first state their positions and interests, then make concessions and adjustments, eventually reach an understanding, and finally write their agreement on paper. According to this view, negotiators talk first and write last. In many situations, however, a negotiating team, as part of its preparation, will reverse this order by drafting a written proposed agreement *before* it actually meets with the other side. A common opening move in their negotiations is to present the other side with a detailed document, known variously as a draft, model, prototype, or standard form contract, to serve as a basis for discussion. Multinational corporations use draft contracts to sell jet aircraft, form joint ventures, and lend money. Governments launch diplomatic initiatives by putting draft treaties on the table. So in practice, negotiators often write first and then talk.

The Aims of the Draft

A draft or model agreement serves many purposes for the side presenting it. First, its preparation is an opportunity for the negotiators representing an organization to consult with important internal and external constituents in order to arrive at an acceptable negotiating position. For example, in preparing to negotiate an automotive joint venture with a Chinese government corporation in China, an international automaker might embody the consensus views of its finance, marketing, engineering, and legal departments in a draft agreement that it would present as a basis of discussion to its potential Chinese partner. Before launching a program to negotiate bilateral investment treaties with developing countries in the 1980s, the United States government took nearly four years to reach a model treaty that was acceptable to concerned U.S. government agencies and departments. This preliminary consultation is not only important preparation for the negotiators themselves, but it also gives them some assurance that any deal that closely follows the draft will be approved by their home office. As we saw earlier, in any negotiation it is important to develop and maintain a mandate when you negotiate for your organization. An agreed-upon form is an important mandate support.

Second, since companies and governments often contemplate similar arrangements with many different parties, a model agreement or standard form contract is an efficient means of informing potential negotiating partners about the type of transaction that the proposing party favors. Uniformity of agreement language also simplifies the administration of numerous similar deals. It can also avoid later charges of discrimination and demands for renegotiation by parties who believe that others have received better treatment than they have. For many companies, like Boeing, beginning all negotiations with the same basic draft is generally seen as a way to make deal making cost-effective and efficient.

A third reason for preparing a formal draft agreement for submission in the negotiation is that it gives the proposing party a tactical advantage. Many experienced negotiators believe that the person who controls the draft controls the negotiation. If the other side accepts the draft as the basis for the discussions, the presenter has in effect set the agenda for the talks and, more important, established the conceptual framework for the deal. To a large extent, the party submitting the draft fixes the terms of reference, while the other side (at least at the outset) is put in the position of merely reacting to the draft's language, rather than advancing specific proposals of its own. Indeed, the party receiving the draft may become so preoccupied with countering the text that it neglects its own negotiating objectives and interests. Thus in my negotiation with the Sudanese, the Egyptian country agreement became an agenda for our discussions and in the end it influenced the content of our agreement with Sudan.

The Perils of the Draft

Although a prepared draft may allow you to control the negotiation, wise negotiators should be careful about applying this bit of conventional advice indiscriminately. Insistence on your own draft may enable you to dominate the negotiation at the beginning, but it may also obstruct agreement in the long run. Effective deal makers should focus on interests, not positions, should search for creative options for mutual gain, and should try to find a formula to accommodate competing goals. Insisting on one's own draft in a negotiation may frustrate these essential goals. For one thing, putting a draft on the table at an early stage in the negotiations may lock parties into bargaining positions, thereby obstructing a search for common interests and creative options. A draft or model agreement is, after all, nothing more than a detailed statement of a position. Then, too, if one of the functions of the early phase of a negotiation is to allow both sides to gather and share as much information as possible about one another, focusing at the outset on the draft is likely to hamper this vital process.

Although corporations may believe that their standard form contracts have universal application, they may in fact be inapplicable to particular local conditions or specific situations under discussion. Consequently, unyielding insistence on their terms may lead to results that are unsatisfactory for both sides. For example, the refusal by an American fast food company to change the language in its master franchise contract requiring the construction of top-quality snow-proof buildings resulted in unnecessarily burdensome building costs for its franchisee in Melbourne, Australia, a city that does not experience heavy snows. So negotiators using an existing standard form should carefully review it before each new negotiation to make sure that its terms are appropriate for the new deal they are trying to make.

Finally, since the party introducing the draft is usually in a superior bargaining position, the other side, like the African officials I mentioned earlier, may view the presentation of the draft as an act of arrogance and a not-too-subtle signal of an unequal relationship between the parties. Consequently, placing a lengthy draft contract on the table at the very beginning of the negotiation may instill suspicion and hostility in the other side, factors that at the very least will slow reaching an agreement and inhibit the development of an effective working relationship with the other side.

All of these reasons suggest that while the preparation of a draft, model, or prototype agreement may be important preparation for a negotiation, negotiators should not automatically introduce that document as an opening gambit in all negotiations. Instead, they should carefully analyze each situation to determine the appropriate time to present their draft in the negotiation process, if at all. They should also recognize that an inflexible insistence on the draft's terms is likely to prolong negotiation and may even derail any chance of an agreement.

Nonetheless, when you are in the often seemingly weak position of negotiating a favor from a government or powerful bureaucracy, presenting a draft authorizing or approving your request can often strengthen your cause. Bureaucrats are busy and may not have a technical grasp of all the details of the issue, so they will often seize on your text as a way of saving time. It is for this reason that a favorite technique of lobbyists for influencing legislation is to put a draft of the desired law, usually written by high-priced Washington law firms, in the hands of legislative staff. You can use the same technique in your daily encounters with the bureaucracies that affect your own life. When an English friend of mine whose son was in a Belgian school but was applying to universities in the U.K. needed to obtain an explanation in English of how the school's grading system related to the one used by English private schools, I suggested that he go to his meeting with the school's headmistress with a draft letter for her signature, providing the necessary explanation. The headmistress immediately took my friend's draft, put it on her letterhead, and sent it off to England the same day. Without the draft, there would have been a delay of several weeks and no assurance that the letter would have been comprehensive enough to satisfy U.K. universities.

Other Written Materials

You may use other written materials, such as memorandums, statements, or briefs, in your negotiations with governments. To the extent that they are persuasive, they also become a type of power tool whose purpose is to influence the decision of the officials sitting across the table from you and later of other persons in the governmental unit who will be involved in deciding on your request. Although the specific nature and content of such documents will depend on the precise subject of the negotiation in which you are engaged, here are a few simple rules that may help make your written materials more persuasive.

1. *Keep it as short as possible.* It is an ancient principle of bureaucracy that short memos get read first and long memos not at all. Remember that the officials with whom you are dealing are busy and in many cases overburdened. To reduce the demands on their time, avoid lengthy documents and carefully scrutinize whatever you present to them for filler, fluff, and verbiage that can be eliminated. In many situations, particularly if you are engaged in legislative lobbying, a one-page memo is the ideal.[2]

2. *State the purpose of your memo or report up front.* In order to allow your counterparts at the table and their colleagues in their governmental unit to become quickly oriented to the significance of your memo report, you should clearly state its purpose as early in the document as possible. A clear introduction, such as "The purpose of this memorandum is . . . ." or "The objective of this report is . . ." lays a vital foundation for what follows.

3. *Get to the point quickly. Don't philosophize.* Having stated the document's purpose, move quickly to discuss the important facts or elements that it deals with. Avoid the temptation to

philosophize about the nature of the problem or to interject material that may be highly interesting but not relevant or helpful to the government official in making a decision on your request.

4. *Use headings and subheadings to structure your document.* Headings and subheadings summarize the main ideas of your report or memorandum. They make initial reading of the document and later reference to particular ideas and points much easier than if the government official had to wade through endless solid blocks of type.

5. *Always use the active voice. Avoid the passive voice.* A memorandum or report written in the active voice reads more easily, sounds more authoritative, and has more punch than one that relies heavily on the passive voice of verbs. Rather than writing "It is believed that . . ." or "Assumptions have been made that . . . ," it is better to state "I believe that . . ." or "We have assumed that . . ."

The Power of No Surprises

At a small luncheon of active and retired government officials, I asked one of them what element was most important for a successful government negotiation. He immediately responded: "No surprises!" All the other heads around the table nodded in unison. When it comes to the functioning of their domains, government officials hate surprises! Surprises often threaten their political positions, particularly surprises that they are not ready to handle. The approval by town regulators of a project that unexpectedly sets off furious community opposition is a surprise. A government contract with one company that provokes a lawsuit by competing companies is a surprise. A regulatory action that generates telephone calls from angry congressional representatives is a surprise. Government officials fear these surprises since they can undermine their political or bureaucratic positions. The element of surprise may be important in a military campaign, but it is rarely effective in negotiating with governments.

You therefore do not want to surprise the government officials you are negotiating with or do things that make them fear a surprise. As a result, before you begin negotiating with particular government officials or agencies, it is a good idea to talk to them informally and let them know what you are planning to do. These initial talks will also give vital information about how to present your application in a way that will maximize your chances of approval. These informal contacts will also provide you important perspectives on the political situation you may be facing and the various politicians and citizens group you may have to include in the process. In my own negotiation in Sudan, my preliminary, informal discussions with aid agencies, Sudanese friends, and foreign diplomats *before* actually sitting down to negotiate the country agreement were indispensable in devising an effective negotiating strategy and in setting the stage for a successful negotiation.

Once you have actually begun negotiations, it is important to alert the officials with whom you are dealing of any factors, positive or negative, that may have a bearing on your proposal. So if you know about potential opposition in the community to the shopping center you are planning, let your government counterparts know about and prepare for it, rather than allow them to be taken by surprise when a delegation of angry neighbors marches into city hall and demands a meeting. If you are lobbying a congressional representative for new legislation, it is best to acknowledge possible negative consequences rather than to pretend they don't exist. Many negotiators like to play "hide the ball" in their business dealings by telling their counterparts as little as possible. Playing this game in a government negotiation, by denying government officials important information that can later cause unpleasant surprises, may get you thrown out of the game for good.

The Power of Prenegotiation

In Chapter 3, we analyzed the negotiation process as having three phases: prenegotiation, conceptualization, and detail arrangement. Many negotiators do not fully use the prenegotiation stage effectively to gather information, identify potential problems, and build relationships with the government department or agency with whom they will be negotiating. Effective prenegotiation is therefore a power tool for influencing the ultimate outcome of your negotiation.

Skillful use of prenegotiation is important in negotiating with all governments—foreign, national, or local. In 1974, when the U.S. federal government offered low-cost loans to build dormitories, Tufts University, part of whose campus lies in the City of Somerville just outside of Boston, secured a loan and obtained permission from the City of Somerville to build a 500-student dormitory. When the community heard about it, it mounted opposition, including protests and lawsuits against Tufts and the city. Faced with this unexpected opposition, the city did nothing to help the university. In fact, it backed away from the project and its officials and politicians ceased to express support. In the end Tufts withdrew the project and never built that particular dormitory. Here then was another example of how a seemingly bilateral negotiation with government over a project suddenly turned into a multilateral activity involving other citizens and groups.

As a result of its experience in 1974, Tufts created a new process for developing new projects that consists basically of four steps:

1. Talk to the mayor first to obtain his views on the project, the right approval process, and the politics of the situation.
2. Go to the closest neighbors to inform them of the University's plans and get their input.
3. Inform more distant neighbors and receive their views.
4. Once a consensus of support has been built, formally apply to the city authorities for the approvals needed.

Other organizations that have failed to follow this approach have had difficulties gaining approval of their projects. A few years ago, the Visiting Nurses Association (VNA), a non-governmental organization in the City of Somerville, bought a property and decided to build a new office building on it. Although the VNA board was advised to talk to the neighbors, it decided not to. It secured a building permit from the city but when news of the project became public it met strong community opposition that stalled the project permanently.

In a case from another state, a grocery chain decided to build a large supermarket in a suburban area that had none. With the aid of consultants and lawyers, it filed a detailed plan that followed the format it had successfully used in other areas. It also hired a public relations firm to get the word to the local media of the advantages to the community of the new supermarket. Hearing that certain residents expressed concern about possible traffic congestion, it commissioned a consulting firm to do a study showing how such problems could be minimized. Despite the significant funds and time that the grocery chain spent on preparing a detailed and complete application, the town authorities refused to grant permission to build the supermarket. While the technical issues involved in planning and developing the project may have led to this result, one also suspects that the authorities were concerned about its potential political impact on the community. They did not want to be surprised by a groundswell of community opposition, so the town authorities simply refused to approve the project.

Before actually beginning negotiations by filing a formal application, the supermarket chain would have been well advised to follow a process similar to that developed by Tufts University. First, company officials should have met informally with local politicians and town planning and public safety officials to inform them about the project and to obtain their suggestions. Second, the grocery chain should have organized community meetings to inform town residents of the new supermarket, to answer their questions, and to receive their concerns. Third, learning that potential traffic problems were a community concern, the company should have proposed to fund a traffic study in which the community and public officials would participate to develop methods to reduce the impact of additional traffic on the town. Fourth, it should have incorporated into its application changes to the original design that would have allowed it to meet objections voiced by the community.[3] Not only would this process have resulted in a project more acceptable to the community, it would also have assured town politicians and officials that their approval of the supermarket project would not lead to unpleasant surprises.

The Power of Relationships

The existence of a positive working relationship between you and your government counterparts will in almost all cases facilitate a negotiation. It can be an important power tool in reaching a desired agreement. In Chapter 4, we saw that Warren Buffett's relationship with Nicholas Brady greatly helped him to reach an agreement that would let Salomon Brothers continue to take part in U.S. Treasury auctions. Lobbyists' relationships with government bureaucrats, congressional members, and their staffs make them effective in negotiating legislative provisions. A relationship is a complex set of interactions characterized by a degree of cooperation and trust between the parties. It implies a sense of *connection* between the parties. As a negotiator with governments, try to build relationships with your government counterparts even before you start negotiations.

It is true that in most of your negotiations with government, you and your government counterpart are merely the representatives of two organizations. Nonetheless, it is important to remember that organizational relationships depend on personal relationships. A genuine relationship cannot exist between two organizations unless persons in each one have a relationship with one another. Similarly, a positive relationship between a company and a government department is usually based on a constructive relationship between the persons involved in negotiating the transaction and then carrying it out. Moreover, to the extent that the negotiators themselves establish a positive relationship with each other, the negotiations are likely to proceed more smoothly and effectively than if no such relationship exists.

Even after the government has signed the contract with you or the administrative agency has granted you the permit you need, continue to maintain and cultivate the relationships that you have developed. Invariably issues will arise in the construction of your project or the execution of your contract that will require you to sit down with your counterparts to work out. Negotiation is not only a tool to create transactions; it is also a means to manage them. To the extent that you have preserved a working relationship with the government department concerned after you have signed the contract or obtained the permit, you will have an easier time of working out the difficulties that may subsequently arise.

The Problem of the Two Cultures

A difference of cultures between government negotiators and their counterparts from the private sector is often an obstacle to relationship building. A government negotiator and a corporate executive may share the same nationality, speak the same language, and live in the same community, but nonetheless represent two distinct professional cultures. What do we mean by culture? Culture consists of the socially transmitted behavior patterns, attitudes, norms, and values of a given community. Persons from that community use the elements of their culture to interpret their surroundings and guide their interactions with other persons.

Culture can therefore be seen as a kind of language, a "silent language" that the parties need in addition to the language they are speaking if they are to arrive at a genuine understanding.[4] Culture serves as a type of social adhesive that binds a group of people together and gives them a distinct identity as a community. It may also give them a sense that they are a community different from other communities. Thus government officials in many cases see themselves as a distinct community from corporate executives, and vice versa. Just as corporate executives exhibit behavior patterns, attitudes, norms, and values that they have gained from their professional community, the same is true of government officials. For example, the behavior patterns, attitudes, and norms and values of corporate executives from New York City who enter into negotiations with town officials in Hope, Arkansas, to build a shopping mall will probably represent two distinct cultures. As a result their interaction may be just as much a cross-cultural negotiation as one between executives of a Dutch oil company and officials of an Arabian Gulf nation. Some sixty years ago, the eminent British novelist and scientist C.P. Snow famously highlighted the breakdown in communications between persons trained in the sciences and those in the humanities as a problem of the "two cultures."[5] You should recognize the difference between government and non-government negotiators as a modern-day version of the problem of Snow's two cultures and should plan negotiations and relationship building accordingly.

Steps in Relationship Building

Relationship building should begin as soon as the two sides have contact with one another. It requires first and foremost mutual knowledge and understanding by the parties. Thus in any negotiation, the negotiators need to get to know each other. The hard and fast rule that some negotiators have of telling the other side as little as possible about themselves and their organizations is not conducive to relationship building or deal making. In other words, you need to get to know the other side and let the other side know you. A policy of "don't ask, don't tell" is not an effective rule for negotiating a working relationship. Indeed, negotiators should do just the reverse: *do* ask and *do* tell.

Do Ask

To build an effective working relationship, the negotiators must know something about each other, not just as organizational representatives but also as people. Relationship building may seem particularly difficult in a negotiation with a government because the negotiators at first may feel that they have very little in common and that matters of status and form—so characteristic of government negotiations—thwart relationship building. Yet differences, if approached wisely, can become a basis for building a relationship.

Cultural and background differences create barriers to relationships. You can work to build a relationship and begin to break down the wall created by cultural differences, not by ignoring them but rather by encouraging the other side to talk about its culture.

By demonstrating sincere interest in the other side's background and culture, a negotiator can begin the process of getting to know the other side. So in a negotiation with the village officials in Hope, Arkansas, the executives from New York City could begin relationship building by showing interest in, knowledge of, and respect for the history of the town, the lifestyle of its people, and the nature of its achievements and its problems. Indeed, failure to show interest in or to ask about the other side in the negotiation can be easily interpreted as an act of cultural superiority and arrogance, a statement that the other side is not significant or important. A working relationship, so essential to the success of any significant transaction, is a complex set of interactions characterized by a degree of cooperation and trust between the parties. Rather than expect the relationship to emerge magically once the contract is signed, the two sides should seek to establish that necessary connection from the very start of their talks.

Do Tell

A further technique in relationship building is to find parallels or similarities between the two sides in the negotiation. Such parallels or similarities may exist between the two organizations, their two cultures, or the two negotiators as individuals. For example, the discovery during the prenegotiation of a proposed joint venture that an American executive and his Swedish counterpart had both studied at the London School of Economics could serve as a first link in building a relationship between the two. Other kinds of shared human experience, both happy and tragic, can facilitate relationship building and ultimately successful negotiation. In the midst of a particularly tense negotiation between Americans and Israelis more than thirty years ago, Prime Minister Golda Meir expressed deep sympathy to one of the U.S. negotiators, whose wife had recently died. Meir referred to the pain she had suffered upon the death of one of her own family members. That brief conversation between the two negotiators improved the negotiating atmosphere dramatically. Meir's expression of sympathy and her reference to a shared tragic experience served to build a personal relationship that led to more productive talks between the American and the Israeli negotiators.[6]

A negotiator should develop nonintrusive ways of inquiring about the other side's background and of encouraging the other side to talk about its background. Questions about culture, when framed in an uncritical way, are messages that say, "Your culture (and therefore you, your people, and your organization) is interesting, important, and worth learning about." Invariably, sincere questions will elicit sincere answers. People like to talk about themselves, and a person's culture and background are very much a part of one's identity. In negotiating with government officials, you need to look beyond their formal titles and public personas to try to understand them as human beings. Once you understand them as human beings, you can begin building effective working relationships.

Often in order to get to know other negotiators and to build a necessary working relationship, you need to let them know you. While a one-on-one encounter should never be dominated by an exposition of your achievements and opinions, the judicious interjection of information about yourself can help to develop a relationship with other persons, a relationship that will make them feel enough trust in you to allow them to reveal important information about their interests and goals.

In his memoir, *Turmoil and Triumph*, former U. S. Secretary of State George Shultz gives a graphic example of how a Russian counterpart at the 1986 Reykjavik Summit between President Ronald Reagan and President Mikhail Gorbachev provided information about himself that led to the development of an effective working relationship between the two sides. In an early meeting with Shultz, Marshal Sergei Akhromeyev, then deputy minister of defense, remarked that he was "one of the last of the Mohegans [sic]," meaning that he was the last of the Soviet World War II commanders still in service. When Shultz asked Akhromeyev where he learned the expression "last of the Mohegans," Akhromeyev replied that he had been raised on the novels of the American writer James Fenimore Cooper. The answer had an immediate impact on Shultz. It led him to conclude that Akhromeyev was more open and ready for conversation than previous Soviet negotiators, that he was a man with a sense of history and an awareness of the American way, and that he was a person the Americans could deal with. "Literature can build bridges," Shultz wrote.[7] As a result, Akhromeyev became Shultz's primary conduit of communication to the Russian side throughout the entire summit.

The Power of Framing

Framing is an important power tool in negotiation. How you frame your request to a government official can often mean the difference between success and failure at the negotiating table. Framing is a process of describing or explaining a situation in a particular way. Framing is the use of analogy, metaphor, or characterization to define the problem or to advocate a solution of that problem. For example, in countries with a suspicion of foreign investment and a strong social welfare tradition, you are more likely to be successful in securing government approval for your project to build a soft drink plant if you characterize it as a "development project" that will yield significant benefits to the community instead of just as a beverage plant that will produce cheap soft drinks and make you a profit.

As a general rule, in any negotiation with a government, always place your proposal within a frame that demonstrates that it is in the public interest. Always justify your demands on public policy grounds, not your personal gain. So if you are lobbying for a tax cut for your industry, you need to frame your proposal as one that would stimulate growth or create jobs, not increase your client's profits. And if you are seeking regulatory relief from an operational restriction that has limited your company's ability to enter a certain field, you will have a greater chance of success if you frame your request as a way to increase competition and thereby improve consumer choices, rather than a means to make more money. Here then is another important difference between negotiating with governments and negotiating with other companies: in the former your chances for success increase with a public policy framework; in the latter they usually don't.

Effective framing is important in a government negotiation for several reasons. First, the government officials on the other side of the table are negotiating within a regulatory or legal framework that specifies the kinds of transactions and approvals they may grant. In order for the officials to be authorized to grant what you seek, you must frame your proposal within the regulatory or legal sphere within which they are operating. Laws and regulations establish frameworks. Actions within the stated framework are permitted. Actions outside the stated framework are not. By proper framing, you put your proposal or request within the stated framework and therefore within the authorized sphere of the official's legitimate activities. Thus, in my negotiations with the Sudanese government, I constantly framed the Ford Foundation's proposed activities as "development activities" and the Foundation as a "development organization" since the office with the friendly diplomat had responsibility for foreign development assistance. Although many of our activities supported education, I did not want to frame our program as educational since then I would have to deal with the Ministry of Education, a less friendly environment than the Ministry of Foreign Affairs.

Second, a frame that convinces your counterparts across the table will probably be the same frame that they use to seek approval from their superiors and to defend against attacks from competing government departments and agencies. Thus, framing the Ford Foundation's activities as developmental would also allow the Ministry of Foreign Affairs to defend their actions against challenges from the Ministry of Education that a Ford Foundation office was subject to its jurisdiction, not the slick diplomats from the foreign ministry down the street.

Third, in view of the fact that any negotiation with the government has the potential to become a matter of public concern involving civic groups and the public in general, the way that you frame the issues can have positive or negative public relations consequences. So always choose your frame with the public in mind. The ability or willingness of the government to support your proposal will depend on having a frame that the government believes it can sell to the public.

Conclusion: Five Rules for Influencing Governments

Despite the seemingly overwhelming power of the government on the other side of the table, you have certain power tools that can increase your chances of influencing a government decision in your favor. As you develop a strategy to conduct your negotiation with a government, keep in mind the following rules for using them:

Rule #1: Always look for a precedent to support your request or proposal. The most influential precedents are those that are specific and relevant to the issue you are negotiating.

Rule #2: Before you actually begin negotiations, consult with officials informally about what you are planning and try to learn as much as you can about the way that particular departments handled similar applications in the past.

Rule #3: Prepare drafts of the agreements you are seeking and introduce them at the proper time in the negotiation.

Rule #4: Frame your proposals in a way that accords with government interests and the political imperatives of your counterparts.

Rule #5: Build relationships with the government officials with whom you will be negotiating and with potentially affected members of the community.

• CHAPTER SEVEN •

Getting a Little Help from Your Friends

Using Third Parties in Government Negotiations

> "What need we have any friends, if we should ne'er have need of 'em? They were the most needless creatures living, if we should ne'er have use for 'em."
>
> —WILLIAM SHAKESPEARE, *TIMON OF ATHENS*

A few years ago, Reebok, the international sports shoe manufacturer, wanted to renegotiate the terms of its contract with one of its major distributors. When the distributor refused, Reebok approached a non-competing manufacturer whose products were also handled by the same distributor and asked it to help persuade the distributor to listen to reason. Fearful that a festering conflict between Reebok and the distributor would have negative consequences for the distribution of its own products, the non-competing manufacturer decided to intervene and ultimately helped Reebok and the distributor arrive at a satisfactory solution to their problem. By involving the non-competing manufacturer, Reebok increased its ability to influence the distributor's decisions in a desired way in order to negotiate a satisfactory agreement. Reebok was successful because it got a little help from a friend.

The Utility of Third Parties

So long as we think that we can achieve our goals on our own, we usually prefer to negotiate deals without the help of others. Involving other people complicates the process and always entails costs. In his negotiations with the U.S. Treasury Department, discussed in Chapter 4, Warren Buffett did not involve a third person but dealt directly with Nicholas Brady, the secretary of the treasury. Buffett certainly felt that he would be more effective in convincing Brady to lift the ban against Salomon Brothers in a conversation involving only the two of them and that the intervention of other persons would have been counterproductive. His relationship with Brady was an important factor in influencing Brady. Its effectiveness would only be diluted if a third party were present.

Indeed, in negotiating situations where we have the upper hand, we not only do not seek the help of others but we also try to prevent the other side from involving third parties on its behalf. In those negotiations, we judge that three is very definitely a crowd. If we believe we are in a dominant position in a negotiation, a bilateral process allows us to apply our power. A multilateral negotiation, on the other hand, has the tendency to dilute our power and reduce our influence, as the Reebok case illustrates with respect to the power wielded by the distributor at the outset of the negotiation. Governments often behave in the same way by trying to limit whom you can bring into a negotiation. If you are negotiating to obtain a permit from a government agency, its rules may specify whom you can bring to the negotiation to help you. If you are a passenger in a car that is stopped for speeding on the highway, the state trooper will make it very clear that your participation is not wanted if you try to involve yourself in the negotiations between the driver and the trooper.

On the other hand, in any human endeavor, whether building a house or waging a war, we tend to seek the help of other persons when the goal seems difficult or impossible to achieve by ourselves.

GETTING A LITTLE HELP FROM YOUR FRIENDS   147

The same phenomenon occurs in negotiations with other persons. Once we come to realize, as Reebok did, that negotiating by ourselves alone may not lead to success, we try to find third parties to involve in the process. We quite naturally look for a little help from our friends.

Faced with what seems the overwhelming power and resources of a government, private parties in government negotiations often sense they need the assistance of third persons if they are to achieve their goals and get what they want from governments. For example, the St. Lawrence Cement Company employed a wide array of third persons in a variety of roles, from lobbyists to lawyers, from public relations consultants to publicists, in seeking permission to build a new cement plant in the Hudson Valley. Despite the legion of third parties under its command, the company failed in its negotiations to obtain the necessary government approvals to build the cement plant. Exxon Mobil, however, was more successful in Africa.

A Little Help with a Pipeline

When Exxon Mobil wanted to undertake a large-scale petroleum development project in Chad with a pipeline through Cameroon to export oil, it encountered ferocious opposition to the project from international environmental and human rights groups because the oil company would be negotiating the deal with two governments that had dubious environmental and human rights records. Exxon Mobil realized that to make the project acceptable to those groups it would have to find a way of assuring them that the project would be managed in a way to benefit the people of those two countries and that its profits would assist in their development and would not find their way to the Swiss bank accounts of the two countries' leaders.

Exxon Mobil knew that all the publicists and public relations firms in the world would not satisfy the project's critics. It also knew that its own promises about fair and effective management of the project and its profits would be scoffed at by the opposition. It needed to find some way to give those promises and statements credibility. To do that, it decided to work to convince the World Bank, an organization with great influence in developing countries, to participate in the project as a lender and to persuade the two governments to give the Bank control over important operational matters, including how some of the profits would be spent.[1] The presence of the Bank in such a key role served to diminish opposition to the project. Without the presence of this crucial third party, Exxon Mobil, still reeling from the costs and negative publicity of the environmental disaster in Alaska caused by its tanker, the *Exxon Valdez*, would not have been able to make the Chad-Cameroon deal in Africa. With the World Bank involved as a participant in the project, opposition receded, and Exxon Mobil and the two countries concerned successfully negotiated an agreement to extract the oil from Chad and to build a pipeline through Cameroon to transport it to the Atlantic Ocean for shipping. Involving a third party, the World Bank, in the negotiation process was essential to making the deal.

Developing a Strategy for Third-Party Intervention in Negotiations

Because of the potentially powerful effect that the presence of a third party may have on any negotiation, you need to think carefully about the strategic choices you will make in this regard. In effect, try to answer four strategic questions:

1. Is there a need to involve other persons or organizations in the negotiations?
2. If so, precisely how should you involve them and what is the precise role you want them to play?
3. What will be the advantages and costs of their involvement in the negotiation process?
4. How will their presence in the negotiation affect the other dynamics of the negotiation process?

You should address these four questions not only at the prenegotiation stage of the negotiation, but throughout the entire process. Your perceived need for a third party may change as the negotiation evolves, so thinking about third-party involvement as a contingency plan is always useful. Thus at the outset, the St. Lawrence Cement Company erroneously thought that the new plant would be easily approved and so it had no need for active third-party involvement. Once public opposition materialized, it, too, had to seek help from third parties just as Exxon Mobil did in Africa.

The Need for a Third Party

The decision about the involvement of a third party in your negotiations with governments will depend first of all on your evaluation of the resources that you need to make the deal with the government agency concerned. This raises two additional questions that you should ask in preparing to negotiate: First, what do I lack to make my negotiation a success? Second, where can I obtain the resources that I lack?

Drawing on the work of social psychologists, one can identify specific bases of influence that a negotiator might use in negotiations to convince the other side to grant what it wants.[2] Six in particular are important. They are:

1. Reward
2. Coercion
3. Expertise and information
4. Relationships
5. Credibility and legitimacy
6. Coalitions and networks

Together, these are a negotiator's assets. In any particular negotiation, the lack of one of these assets may prevent you from reaching the agreement that you want. In that case, you need to see if a third party can provide it at a cost that you are willing to pay.

Let's see how these assets will work for you.

1. *Rewards.* The promise of rewards or benefits to be gained from an envisioned agreement is often what causes the other side

in a negotiation to agree to your proposal. Governments, like private parties, also seek to gain rewards from their negotiations, but as we discussed in Chapter 2, individual governments and departments may have their own special way of calculating rewards. For example, the expectation of a reward for Sudan in the form of increased development assistance was an important factor in securing a country agreement for the Ford Foundation.

In some negotiations, you may discover that you do not have sufficient resources to give the other side the reward it is seeking. For example, a government may not be willing to enter into a vehicle supply contract with you because it judges that your plant's capacity is incapable of producing the required number of vehicles per month necessitated by government plans. Instead of ending negotiations, you might look for another company that can help you provide the rewards that the government is seeking and form a joint venture with that company to negotiate for the government contract in hopes that your combined production capacity will satisfy government demands.

2. *Coercion.* The threat of loss or punishment is another basis that influences the decisions of other persons at the negotiating table. Often the inclusion of the appropriate third party can lend credibility and heft to such a threat. For example, in a negotiation with a government agency that has broken its contract with you, your threat to sue gains more credence if you involve a noted litigation law firm as part of your team. Similarly, your threat to challenge the denial of a regulatory permit from a government agency becomes more powerful if you hire as your lobbyist a former congressional representative who has a close relationship to the chair of the congressional committee having oversight over the agency that denied the permit.

3. *Information and Expertise.* Information and expertise are vital assets in any negotiation. Your lack of information and expertise, for example about regulations, precedents, and procedures, may prevent you from obtaining a government permit to build a shopping center or a motorcycle racetrack. One of the assets that lobbyists and Washington lawyers give you is the exper-

tise necessary to pursue that permit successfully. Tommy Corcoran, the legendary Washington lobbyist, described his primary function in this light when he testified before a senate committee that was looking into the problem of "influence peddling" within the federal government: "I do not know, and I feel quite sure no one else knows just what 'influence' means. If with respect to me it means experience in knowing what government likes and does not like, I cannot understand why it should not be used to make the burden of government lighter."[3]

Lobbyists as government helpers? One is tempted to dismiss Corcoran's statement in defense of lobbying as a cynical attempt to put a public service justification on what is fundamentally a self-serving activity. On the other hand, Corcoran's testimony does offer an important insight that explains why the intervention of a third party is sometimes effective in negotiations with government departments and agencies, an insight that may be useful in shaping your own strategies and tactics. Government departments are often busy, understaffed, and burdened by heavy demands. Moreover, they often do not have the full range of expertise that is necessary for making certain decisions required of them. Lobbyists are effective with those departments because they have that expertise. By providing it in readily usable form, often with a draft law or regulation attached, they are able to influence government officials by making their jobs easier. Accordingly, in your negotiations with government, follow Corcoran's advice and seek to make presentations and provide information in ways that lighten that government department's burdens.

Lobbyists are not the only ones who bring needed expertise and information to a government negotiation and thus facilitate agreements with private parties. In one negotiation between the government of Trinidad and Tobago and Tesoro Petroleum Company, an American corporation, the two parties were deadlocked over how to divide profits of nearly $150 million from their joint venture to develop and manage oil fields in Trinidad. Tesoro sought an outright distribution of its share of the profits so that it might develop oil-producing properties elsewhere in the world.

The government of Trinidad and Tobago wanted the joint venture to reinvest its profits in Trinidad.

Unable to reach agreement and nearing the point of suing each other in arbitration, the two sides asked Lord Wilberforce, a distinguished retired English judge, to serve as their conciliator. After listening to the parties, Lord Wilberforce delivered them a lengthy written report, in which he stated that his task as a conciliator had three dimensions: (1) to examine the contentions raised by the parties; (2) to clarify the issues in dispute; and (3) to evaluate the respective merits of the parties' positions and the likelihood of their prevailing in arbitration. Thus, he saw his task as giving the parties a prediction of their fate in arbitration, with the hope that such prediction would assist them in negotiating a settlement. He concluded his report with a suggested settlement based on his estimate of the parties' chances of success in arbitration on the issues in dispute. Within a few months Tesoro and the Trinidad and Tobago government negotiated a settlement providing for a division of the profits of their joint venture. It was the introduction of the information and expertise of Lord Wilberforce into the negotiation process that gave the parties the assets they needed to make a deal.[4]

4. *Relationships.* In Chapter 4, we discussed the importance of access in penetrating and engaging a government department in a negotiation, and we noted that a preexisting relationship between a private party and the government agency is often vital in effecting such access. Warren Buffett had access to U.S. Treasury Secretary Nicholas Brady because of an existing relationship so he did not need to seek help from a third party. But many private persons and companies lack the necessary access, so they turn to persons, like lobbyists, lawyers, and politicians, who can provide this important—indeed crucial—element for any successful negotiation.

A third party's relationships can provide more than access to begin a negotiation. They can also serve as a means of influence. One of the most effective ways to increase your power in a negotiation is to build supportive relationships with a strong third party who may be willing to intervene on your side in the negotiation. Thus in my negotiations in the Sudan, I encouraged the heads of institutions with which the Ford Foundation had been working to contact the Ministry of Foreign Affairs and urge it to negotiate a country agreement that would facilitate the Foundation's work there.

5. *Credibility and Legitimacy.* In any negotiation, the credibility of the negotiators is an important asset. Whether the other side believes or disbelieves your statements and commitments can mean the difference between making a deal and losing it. Similarly, the fact that you as a negotiator have legitimacy as the proper representative of a group is also an important asset. In situations where a government agency does not believe that you have credibility or legitimacy, the introduction of an appropriate third party can help you gain these important assets. Thus in the Chad-Cameroon pipeline case, Exxon Mobil did not have sufficient credibility or legitimacy to make a deal that would not be the subject of strong opposition. The introduction of the World Bank as a lender and participant in the project gave it sufficient credibility and legitimacy to dampen that opposition. Also, one of the ways to gain access is to have a third party known and respected by the government department introduce you to the government department, thereby implicitly giving you the credibility and legitimacy to negotiate with it.

6. *Alliances and Coalitions.* In many situations, we select a third party to assist us not only because of the relationship that person may have with counterparts on the other side of the table but also because of its relationships with groups that may have influence with the government department with which we are negotiating. In short, that third party by its presence brings those alliance and coalitions to the table. For example, using a lobbyist who is a Republican to work the Republican side of the legislature and another who is a Democrat to work the Democratic side, as one Minnesota public institution routinely does to secure its annual budget, is mobilizing those alliances and networks on its behalf in its budgetary negotiations. Each lobbyist uses those party

alliances and affiliations as instruments of influence in its negotiations with the legislators concerned.

Third-Party Roles

Having decided that you need a particular third party because of certain important assets that it possesses, you next have to decide in what role you want to involve that third party in your negotiations. The precise role played is important because it can affect the extent to which that third party is able to inject into the negotiation the asset that he or she possesses and that you lack. It also affects the costs of securing that third party's help. The possible range of role options for third persons is extensive. Here are a few:

1. *Advisor.* A third person may merely serve as your advisor in the negotiations, providing you with knowledge and expertise that you lack. A lawyer with expertise in land use regulation in a particular city may work with you in securing the building permit for a shopping center. Your choice of a particular firm as your advisor in a given negotiation may be driven not only by its knowledge and expertise but by other factors as well. The advisor may have relationships with the government agency that give you access to that agency. In addition, the choice of one advisor instead of another may serve as a signal to the government department of your intentions, policies, and level of resources. For example, hiring an environmental consulting firm that has a reputation for making particularly rigorous environmental impact assessments is a communication to the government department concerned that you are serious about meeting environmental standards. On the other hand, hiring a firm that has a reputation for cutting corners in its environmental assessments conveys just the opposite message. So in deciding on your advisors you should try to learn how they are viewed by the government department with which you are negotiating. A further tactical decision is whether that advisor may either be part of your negotiating team at the talks or work for you only behind the scenes. Will the presence of a large negotiating team impress the government department with your re-

sources or will it instead view your approach as threatening and therefore make it defensive?

2. *Negotiation Support.* In this role, the third person may undertake a variety of tasks in support of your negotiation, such as public relations, translation, media relations, or research. It is well to remember that you need to manage and monitor these supporting services carefully, for they can complicate and even impede an otherwise effective negotiation if they are not made part of an integrated process.

3. *Negotiating Agent.* A third person may negotiate on your behalf with the government department concerned. Thus, your land use lawyer may actually conduct the negotiations to obtain the permit you are seeking from a zoning board. Whether your lawyer should actually negotiate on your behalf, or just be confined to giving you advice, will depend not only on his knowledge of the law, but whether that person has the necessary negotiating skills to get you what you want.

4. *Lobbyist.* Lobbyists have become a permanent part of the process by which private parties seek significant action from the legislative and executive branches of government. Some lobbyists are engaged especially for a major action, such as favorable revision of Medicare legislation. Some are on contract or retainer to watch over and advance a client's interests, for example in the case of a university, to make sure that it obtains favorable "earmarks" in legislation to fund particular projects, such as laboratories or dormitories. Still others work on salary for trade associations, like the American Trucking Association, special interest groups, like the American Association of Retired Persons (AARP), and civic groups, like Common Cause. Yet others work for the government relations offices of individual companies and organizations.[5]

5. *Ally.* Developing alliances and coalitions of persons and organizations that support your position in your negotiation with a government is an important tool of influence. Allies in these coalitions and alliances are rarely at the negotiating table with you but they can still exert influence on your government counterparts on

your behalf. For example, in many negotiations with governments, you may want to line up congressional representatives, senators, or state legislators in support of your position. They may take various positions as your ally, from advocating your case strenuously with the government department concerned to simply making a polite inquiry as to the status of negotiations.

Before selecting an ally, you need to analyze the network of persons and institutions that have influence with the government department or agency concerned and the basis of influence that such persons and organizations exert. While some may have influence because they are supporters or constituents of that department, others are influential because they are powerful adversaries feared by the department. Still others are significant neutrals who have some other basis of influence such as a distinguished reputation or a powerful network of their own.

Probably the option with the greatest risk is to select as an ally an adversary of the government department concerned. That choice may indeed sometimes wring concessions from a weak government department, but it may also provoke its hostility and increase its determination to dominate the situation because it now faces what it considers to be a genuine threat. This approach may get you the permit or authorization you are seeking *this time*. But in the future, as alliances change and power shifts, as they inevitably do in government, you may find your self paying dearly for this short-term victory. Remember, government bureaucracies never forget and they hardly ever forgive. On the other hand, raising the specter of a competitor, without actually involving it in the conflict, can be an effective form of influence as it was for many small countries during the cold war. A friend of the other side is usually the most appropriate third party, as long as that third party does not merely seek to hand over the weak party to the adversary. By virtue of their friendly relationship, the third party has the ability to influence the other side toward an acceptable solution.

Once you have identified a potential ally, you must then analyze its interests in supporting you. In effect, you may have to conduct a separate negotiation with allies in order to persuade them to join your alliance. And finally, once they do join you, remember that no alliance is forever. You need to make efforts to maintain that alliance, for example by staying in contact with your allies and keeping them informed about developments in your negotiation with the government department or agency.

6. *Participant.* In order to secure certain negotiating assets, you may have to persuade a third party to become a participant in the transaction you are trying to negotiate. Thus, the only way the World Bank could bring its legitimacy and credibility to the Chad-Cameroon pipeline deal was to join it as a participant.

7. *Mediator.* Like Lord Wilberforce, third parties can often aid a negotiation when they play the role of independent mediators whose aim is to help both sides to arrive at a mutually acceptable agreement. Here, in addition to their expertise, their independence and impartiality are important assets. Thus, Tesoro Petroleum and the Trinidad and Tobago government could use Lord Wilberforce's report as a basis of agreement not only because of the expertise he brought to the issue but also because he exercised that expertise impartially, independent of the two parties in the dispute. A similar approach may help you in particularly conflicted negotiations with a government. For example, if you and the school board are stuck over the terms for the sale of an abandoned school, you might suggest to the school board that you both invite into your discussion a distinguished and independent expert or political leader to mediate your dispute and help you both arrive at an agreement that meets both your needs.

8. *Arbitrator.* In certain situations, where the parties cannot agree on one or more issues, they may consent to submit the matter to a mutually acceptable third party, an arbitrator, and agree to abide by that third party's decision. Many contracts between governments and foreign companies specially provide for arbitration in the event of a dispute relating to their contract. For example, in the dispute between Tesoro and the government of Trinidad and Tobago, the parties could have asked Lord Wilberforce to make a binding decision on how to share profits, rather than to mediate with a recommended settlement.

The Costs of Third-Party Intervention

In negotiations as in life, choosing your friends carefully is important. No third party is an altruist. The intervention of a third party into your negotiations with a government always has a cost. You should always evaluate those costs and determine whether you are prepared to pay them in light of the expected benefit you hope to receive in the negotiation. That cost may be paid in a variety of currencies, including money, time, autonomy, and future obligations.

The costs of third-party help in a government negotiation take several forms. The first and most obvious cost is monetary. Lobbyists, lawyers, and public relations firms don't come cheap. Each year U.S. companies spend billions of dollars to retain their services in negotiations with governments at all levels.

The intervention of a third party may also entail substantial organizational costs. The involvement of third parties in the negotiation process always requires management on your part to make sure that lawyers, lobbyists, allies, and agents are all working effectively together to achieve the goals you are seeking. In negotiating to acquire the abandoned school, it is important that your agents at the table, your public relations firm, and your lobbyists at city hall are giving a consistent message, because inconsistencies will be exploited by your opponents as proof of insincerity and even duplicity. In managing third parties, it is important to remember that third parties always pursue their own interests, even when they claim to work on behalf of other parties, and the pursuit of those interests may complicate and even obstruct the negotiation process. For example, if your lobbyist does a lot of business with a particular government department, consider how the expectation of future dealings with that department may affect the way your lobbyist is advancing your cause today.

Similarly, the non-competing manufacturer was willing to intervene in Reebok's dispute with its distributor because it feared that Reebok's continuing conflict would have a negative effect on the distributor's ability to sell the non-competing manufacturer's own goods. A *competing* manufacturer might have refused to undertake the task or have done it in such a way as to disadvantage Reebok.

Involving certain third parties may entail no costs immediately but they may have substantial future costs. Allies who help you with a government agency today may look for assistance from you in the future on some other matter. Be sure that you are willing to pay those costs before you invite them into your negotiation.

Choosing and Watching Your Friends

How then can you be absolutely sure that a third party will truly act in your interests in a negotiation and not use it in some way to advance its own interests? The short answer to that question is that, of course, you can't. However, you can increase the chances that a third party will work to get what you want if you spend time on three essential aspects: (1) selection; (2) interest alignment; and (3) monitoring. First, select any third party with care, making sure that it has the range of resources and experience that you need. Second, understand the interests of that third party and how those interests may affect your negotiation. For example, if you form a joint venture with another company to obtain a government contract, evaluate the likelihood that the other company will eventually force you out of the deal and take over the contract itself in the future. Try to develop arrangements that will align that third party's interest with your own interests. And finally, try to keep an eye on your friends. Monitor what they are doing. This means that you have to stay in contact with them and receive regular reports.

Conclusion: Four Rules for Getting a Little Help from Your Friends

Rule #1: The right third party can help you get what you want from a government in a negotiation.

Rule #2: Before seeking help, identify the resources you lack in a negotiation and decide who can provide them. Some resources that you need and that a third party can provide include rewards, coercion, expertise and information, relationships, credibility and legitimacy, and alliances and coalitions.

Rule #3: When you have identified the friend who can provide what you need, decide on the particular role that you would like that person to play in your negotiation. Possible roles include advisor, support, agent, lobbyist, ally, participant, mediator, and arbitrator.

Rule #4: No third-party intervention is free. Always evaluate the costs of any third-party intervention that you are contemplating and decide whether the benefit it brings is worth the cost. Make sure you understand the interests of that third person and do what you can to make its interest align with yours.

• CHAPTER EIGHT •

The Deal Is Never Done

Renegotiating Government Agreements

"Issues are never settled in this town."

—FORMER SECRETARY OF STATE GEORGE P. SHULTZ[1]

Despite lengthy negotiations, skilled drafting, and strict enforcement mechanisms, parties to solemnly signed and sealed agreements often find themselves returning to the bargaining table later on to renegotiate their agreements. So a key challenge in negotiating any agreement is not just getting to yes, but also staying there.

The Tragedy of Life Struggling Against Form

The renegotiation of existing agreements is a constant in all areas of life. Economic recessions or significant changes in prices invariably lead to restructurings and workouts of thousands of negotiated arrangements made in better times. Companies facing financial crises sometimes try to find a solution to their problems by renegotiating their labor contracts. At the international level, we have witnessed the renegotiation of mineral and petroleum agreements in the 1960s and 1970s, often in the face of threatened host country nationalizations and expropriations. We have seen the loan reschedulings of the 1980s following the debt crisis in developing countries and the restructuring of project and financial agreements as a result of the Asian financial crisis of the late 1990s.

The risk of renegotiation of apparently definitive agreements is particularly present in dealings with governments for a variety of reasons. Governments often reserve to themselves the right to unilaterally change contracts on grounds of protecting national sovereignty, national security, or the public welfare. Moreover, the usual remedies in court for breach of contract may be unavailable or ineffectual against governments who take such actions. As we have seen, governments are particularly susceptible to political forces in their negotiations with private persons and companies. The changing nature of the political imperatives under which governments labor can cause them to change their position on agreements that they have previously made. Throughout the world, from Albany to Zanzibar, when political opposition develops toward agreements that governments have made, at some point, when the pressure becomes too great to resist, those governments will look for ways to cancel or redo those agreements in order to satisfy their political constituents. Former Secretary of State George Shultz was right when he said that in government "it's never over," that issues and agreements are hardly ever settled once and for all.

In today's uncertain and changing world, executives, lawyers, and government officials seem to be constantly seeking to renegotiate, either to alleviate a bargain that has become onerous or to hold on to a good deal that the other side wants to change. The examples are so numerous that *re*negotiating existing agreements seems as basic to human relations as is negotiating new agreements for the first time. More than seventy-five years ago, Karl Llewellyn, a noted American legal scholar, captured the tension between negotiated agreements and subsequent reality in the conclusion of his thoughtful inquiry into the role of contract in the social order: "One turns from the contemplation of the work of contract as from the experience of Greek tragedy. Life struggling against form . . ."[2] Renegotiation is one of the most important theaters in which parties to existing agreements play out the continuing struggle of life against form. Because of its prevalence in dealings with governments, negotiators need to understand the forces that give rise to renegotiation, the nature of the renegotiation process, and the best ways to renegotiate deals that they thought were done.

Defining Renegotiation

The term "renegotiation" applies to three fundamentally different situations, and it is therefore important at the outset for negotiators to understand the distinctions among the three. Each situation raises different problems, and each demands different solutions. The three situations are: *post-deal* renegotiations, *intra-deal* renegotiations, and *extra-deal* renegotiations.

Post-Deal Renegotiations

Post-deal renegotiation refers to the situation in which negotiations take place at the expiration of a contract when the two sides, though legally free to go their own way, nonetheless try to renew their relationship. For example, a power company has built an electrical generating station and has made a twenty-year contract to supply electricity to a state public utility. At the end of twenty years, when local law considers their legal relationship at an end, the power company and the public utility begin discussions on a second long-term electricity supply contract, thereby "renegotiating" their original relationship. While this second negotiation process—a post-deal renegotiation—may seem at first glance to resemble the negotiation of their original contract, it also has some notable differences, as we shall see, that influence renegotiation strategies, tactics, and outcomes.

Intra-Deal Renegotiations

A second type of renegotiation occurs when the agreement itself provides that during its life at specified times or on the happening of specified events the parties may renegotiate or review certain the agreement's provisions. For example, the twenty-year electricity supply contract mentioned above might include a provision calling for the renegotiation of the agreement's pricing terms in the event of dramatic changes in fuel costs. Here renegotiation is anticipated as a legitimate activity in which both parties, while still bound to each other in a valid contract, are to engage in good faith. It is an intra-deal renegotiation because it takes place within the legal framework established for the original transaction.

Extra-Deal Renegotiations

The most difficult, stressful, and emotional renegotiations are those undertaken in apparent violation of the contract or at least in the absence of a specific clause authorizing a renegotiation. These negotiations take place "extra deal," for they occur outside the framework of the existing agreement. The negotiations to reschedule loans following the Third World debt crisis of the early 1980s, the effort by the American government to renegotiate the ABM Treaty with the Russians in 2001, and attempts by companies to secure changes in existing union contracts all fit within the category of extra-deal renegotiations. In each case, one of the participants is seeking relief from a legally binding obligation without any basis for renegotiation in the agreement itself.

Negotiation and Renegotiation Are Different

All three types of renegotiation are a constant and ever-present fact of contemporary life. Yet three important factors distinguish them from negotiations in first instance and significantly affect the renegotiation process:

1. Increased mutual knowledge
2. Increased transactional understanding
3. Increased mutual linkage

First, as a result of working together during their first agreement, the parties know much more about each other than when they first negotiated their agreement. Second, many of the questions that they had about their contemplated transaction during their initial negotiation have now been answered. And third, as a result of their investments in the transaction during their first agreement, it may now be more costly to abandon renegotiations than it was to have walked away from their initial negotiations

At the same time, in each of these three types of renegotiation different relationships and processes are at work. These factors lead to different strategies and tactics that negotiators may employ. Let's now explore in detail the processes at work in the three kinds of renegotiation.

Post-Deal Renegotiations

Post-deal renegotiations happen often in government relationships since government permissions, licenses, and contracts are normally for a limited period of time but usually provide for the possibility of renewal. The renewal process is the most common form of post-deal renegotiation.

Distinguishing Factors

Although post-deal renegotiations take place when the original transaction has reached or is approaching its end, several factors distinguish it from a negotiation in first instance, factors that may significantly affect the renegotiation process. First, by virtue of law, custom, or express or implied contractual commitments, the parties may have a legal obligation to negotiate in good faith with one another despite the fact that their original contract has terminated; consequently, their ability to refuse to engage in post-deal renegotiations may be limited. The existence and precise nature of such a duty will depend on the law governing the contract.

Anglo-American law has traditionally recognized a broad, unrestrained freedom of negotiation that permits a party to begin or end negotiation at any time for any reason.[3] The rationale for this rule is that a limitation on the freedom to negotiate might discourage persons from undertaking transactions in the first place. By contrast, the law in certain other countries is less liberal, holding that once the parties have commenced negotiations, they may have an obligation to negotiate in good faith.[4]

But even in common law countries, the parties may have an obligation to renegotiate an agreement in good faith at its end because of an express provision in the original contract, the prevailing practices and customs of the business concerned, or the conduct of the parties toward one another during the life of their agreement. In contrast, parties seeking to negotiate a transaction in first instance would have no such obligation and could abandon negotiations at any time.

The precise content of the obligation to negotiate in good faith varies from country to country. It may include a duty not to negotiate with a third person until post-deal negotiations with a party in the original transaction have failed. It may also require a party not to terminate renegotiations without reasonable cause and without having persevered for a reasonable length of time. Failure by either side to fulfill its obligations to renegotiate in good faith may result in liability in damages.

Even if the applicable law imposes no legal obligation to renegotiate in good faith, the original contract, as well as economic factors, may constrain the post-deal renegotiation process in ways not present in the original negotiations. For example, the twenty-year electricity supply contract mentioned above might provide that if the power company and the public utility fail to negotiate a second twenty-year supply contract, the public utility company will be obligated to purchase the project company's electrical generating station according to a pricing formula specified in the original agreement.

Beyond legal and contractual constraints, the three factors mentioned above—the parties' increased mutual knowledge, increased transactional understanding, and increased mutual linkage—will significantly influence the course of negotiations. For example, in renegotiating the electricity supply agreement, the power company's approach will be more cautious and reluctant if the history of the first contract was plagued by late and contested payments than if the public utility had always paid on time and in full. Similarly, if over the first twenty years the price of power under the contract had proven to be much higher than competing forms of energy, the public utility would seek reductions in the pricing formula during the renegotiation. And finally, the fact that the power company organized itself and trained its employees to provide electricity over the long term to a single specific purchaser will probably mean that all other things being equal, the power company would prefer to enter into a new contract with the utility, rather than to make an agreement with another purchaser, a course of action entailing significant new risks and costs. Then too, the public utility, having come to rely on the power company for a major portion of its electrical supply, may wish to avoid the costs of finding another supplier or creating its own electrical generating capacity.

In any negotiation, a party's actions at the negotiating table are influenced by its evaluation of available alternatives to the deal it is trying to negotiate. Rational negotiators will not ordinarily agree to an outcome that is inferior to their best alternative. In a post-deal renegotiation, each party's evaluation of its alternatives will be heavily influenced by its knowledge of the other side obtained during the first agreement, its understanding of the transaction gained during that time, and the extent of the investment that it has made in the relationship.

In general, the success of post-deal renegotiations will depend on the nature of the relationship that has developed between the parties during the original contract. If that relationship has been strong and productive, the atmosphere at the bargaining table will be that of two partners trying to solve a common problem. However, if the relationship has been weak and troubled, the prevailing mood will be that of two cautious adversaries who know each other only too well.

Three Principles to Guide Post-Deal Renegotiations

The factors discussed above give rise to the following principles that you should consider in structuring and conducting the process of post-deal renegotiation.

1. *Provide for post-deal renegotiations in the original contract.* In transactions in which the desirability or likelihood of post-deal renegotiations is high, the parties should specify in their original agreement the process and rules that they will follow in conducting a post-deal renegotiation. For example, the contract should state how soon before the end of the contract renegotiations are to begin, how long the renegotiations are to continue before either party may legally abandon them, where the renegotiations are to take place, and the nature of the information that each side is to provide the other, among other matters. Recognizing that post-deal renegotiations may become problematic, the contract might also authorize the use of mediators or other third-party helpers in the process.

2. *Individually and jointly review the history of the relationship during the original contract.* As part of its preparation, each party to a post-deal renegotiation should review carefully and thoroughly the experience of working with the other side during the first contract. An understanding of the problems encountered during that period will enable each side to shape proposals to remedy them during a contemplated second agreement. To make that review an opportunity for creative problem solving rather than mutual acrimony over past mistakes, the parties should structure a joint review of past experience, perhaps with the help of a neutral facilitator, at the beginning of the post-deal renegotiation process. For example, as a first step in the renegotiation process, the power company and the public utility might give a review team, consisting of executives from the company and officials from the public utility, the task of preparing a mutually acceptable history of their relationship. Inevitably, during the course of post-deal renegotiations, each side will refer to past events. The renegotiation process will proceed more smoothly and efficiently if at the beginning of the process the parties have a common understanding of their history together than if they engage in a continuing debate throughout the renegotiation about the existence and significance of past events.

3. *Understand thoroughly the alternatives to a renegotiated deal.* Negotiators should not only evaluate their own alternatives

to the deal that they are trying to make but they should also try to estimate their counterparts' alternatives. In a post-deal renegotiation, these two tasks are often complicated by the fact that the parties may have conducted their activities in such a way during the first contract that few realistic alternatives to a second contract seem possible. For example, the power company that owns a generating facility may feel that it has few other options than to enter into a second contract with the state public utility. Or the public utility company in a time of energy shortage may see no realistic alternatives to making a second electricity power purchase agreement with the power company. Rather than accepting the inevitability of a second contract, each side, long before the termination of the first contract, should carefully examine all options and seek to develop possible new alternatives before entering into post-deal renegotiations with the other side. For example, the state public utility, perhaps several years in advance of the end of the first contract, might contact other potential project companies to determine their interest in developing electrical generation plants.

Intra-Deal Renegotiations

Intra-deal renegotiation happens particularly in long-term arrangements. Its purpose is to enable the parties to overcome their inability at the time they negotiate their original contract to predict important events affecting their relationship in the future.

Balancing Contractual Stability and Change

A goal sought by all sides in any negotiation is contractual stability—the assurance that the terms of their agreement will be respected in the future. At the same time, the parties know that during the period of their agreement unforeseen events may arise to change drastically the balance of benefits originally contemplated from their agreement. Consequently, a fundamental challenge in contracting practice is to achieve contractual stability and at the same time allow the parties to deal with changing circumstances in the future. The traditional approach to resolving this dilemma is for the parties during their original negotiation to attempt to anticipate all possible contingencies and to provide solutions for them in their agreement. This approach rejects the idea of intra-deal renegotiation.

Another solution to the problem of balancing the imperatives of stability and change is for the contract itself to authorize the parties to renegotiate key elements of their relationship upon the happening of specified events or circumstances. In view of the impossibility of predicting all possible future contingencies, the inclusion in the agreement of some type of intra-deal renegotiation clause would appear to be a useful device to give needed flexibility to long-term agreements. In fact, however, companies do not frequently use them.

The traditional reluctance to use renegotiation clauses stems from a variety of factors, both legal and practical. First is the concern among lawyers that renegotiation clauses are merely "agreements to agree" and therefore may be unenforceable. On the other hand, although the English common law has tended to dismiss agreements to negotiate as unenforceable, the contemporary approach in most American courts is to enforce agreements to negotiate in good faith.[5] It would seem that a specific renegotiation clause in an existing contract with definite terms as to how the parties are to conduct the renegotiation process would easily meet this standard of enforceability. The required certainty would be further satisfied by specifying the precise events that give rise to the obligation to renegotiate and by specifically providing for the timing, locale, and conditions of the renegotiation process, among others.

Practical considerations have also led western executives to view renegotiation clauses with suspicion on grounds that they increase uncertainty and risk in transactions and offend western concepts of the sanctity of contract. Their presence in a contract also creates a risk that one of the parties will use a renegotiation clause as a lever to force changes in provisions that strictly speaking are not open to revision. The challenge of drafting these provisions and the heightened risks to contractual stability by renegotiation clauses that have yet to be tested in the courts are additional factors that have deterred their use in long-term contracts.

Despite these potential pitfalls, the inclusion of a renegotiation clause may actually contribute to transactional stability in certain situations. First, in cases in which significant changes in circumstances may result in severe unexpected financial hardship, a renegotiation clause may permit the parties to avoid default, with the attendant risk of litigation and extra-deal renegotiations. During the original negotiations, it may be wiser for the parties to recognize the risk of changed circumstances and create within the contract a process to deal with them rather than to try to predict all eventualities and then be subject to the uncertain decisions of courts when those predictions prove to be flawed.

A second situation in which a renegotiation clause may be helpful occurs in cases in which the parties, by virtue of their differing cultures, understand and perceive the basis of their transaction in fundamentally different ways. For example, western notions of business transactions as being founded upon law and contract often clash with Asian conceptions of business arrangements as based on personal relationships. In Asia, executives often consider the essence of a business deal to be the relationship between the parties, rather than the written contract, which in their view can only describe that relationship imperfectly and incompletely. They may also assume that any long-term business relationship includes an implicit, fundamental principle: in times of change, parties in a business relationship should decide together how to cope with that change and adjust their relationship accordingly.

The western party, on the other hand, may view the transaction as set in the concrete of a lengthy and detailed contract without the possibility of modification while the Asian side may see the transaction as floating on the parties' fluid personal relationships, which always have within them an implicit commitment to renegotiate the terms of the transaction in the event of unforeseen happenings. In such long-term transactions, for example between a western energy company and an Asian government, whose success depends on close and continuing cooperation, it may be wise to recognize this difference of view at the outset of negotiations and attempt to find some middle ground. A renegotiation clause may represent such middle ground between total contractual rigidity on the one hand and complete relational flexibility on the other. It recognizes the possibility of redoing the deal, but controls the renegotiation process. An intra-deal renegotiation clause, then, may give stability to an arrangement whose long-term nature creates a high risk of instability.

Approaches to Intra-Deal Renegotiation

In recent years, the use of renegotiation clauses in long-term agreements seems to have become somewhat more frequent.[6] A variety of intra-deal renegotiation clauses exists to cope with the challenge of balancing the need for contractual stability with the need for a means to adapt agreements to drastic changes in circumstances. Here are some of the principal types that you may wish to consider in your own contracts with government authorities:

1. *The Implicit Minor Renegotiation Clause.* Despite some lawyers' claims to the contrary, contracts in long-term arrangements, no matter how detailed, are not a kind of comprehensive instruction booklet that the parties follow blindly. At best, such agreements are *frameworks* within which the participants constantly adjust their relationship. Karl Llewellyn underscored this point more than seventy-five years ago:

> The major importance of a legal contract is to provide a frame-work for well-nigh every type of group or organization and for well-nigh every type of passing or permanent relation between individuals and groups, up to and including states—a frame-work highly adjustable, a frame-work which almost never accurately indicates real working relations, but which affords a rough indication around which such relations vary, an occasional guide in cases of doubt, and a norm of final appeal when the relations cease in fact to work.[7]

Executives responsible for implementing long-term transactions have consistently confirmed Llewellyn's observation in similar terms: "Once the contract is signed, we put it in the drawer," they have frequently told me. "After that what matters most is the relationship between us and our partner, and we are negotiating that relationship all the time." What this view means in practice is that certain matters in the agreement, usually but not always of a minor nature, are subject to renegotiation by the parties as part of their ongoing relationship, despite the fact that their contract contains no specific renegotiation clause. One can therefore argue that an "implicit minor renegotiation clause" is part of any transaction agreement. For example, if the electrical supply agreement in the example above provides that the project is to commence delivery of electricity on July 1, 2008, but it later develops that a four-day national holiday is to fall on that date, making it difficult for the public utility to accept delivery, the parties would renegotiate a more appropriate time for delivery.

2. *Review Clauses*. Long-term contracts, particularly in the oil and mineral industries, sometimes commit the parties to meet at specific times to "review" the operation of their agreement. For example, one mining agreement with a government provided that the parties were to meet together every seven years "with a view to considering in good faith whether this Agreement is continuing to operate fairly to each of them and with a view further to discussing in good faith any problems arising from the practical operation of this agreement."[8] Although the words "negotiation" or "renegotiation" appear nowhere in the clause, one reasonable interpretation of the provision is that it carries an implicit obligation for the parties to resolve problems through good faith negotiation.

3. *Automatic Adjustment Clauses*. Transaction agreements often contain certain terms, such as those concerning prices or interest rates, subject to automatic change by reference to specified indices, such as a cost of living index or the London Interbank Offered Rate (LIBOR). For example, the electricity supply contract we have been discussing might link the price to be paid for the electricity by the public utility to variations in fuel costs or the

local cost of living index. While the aim of such a provision is to provide for flexibility without the risks inherent in renegotiation, negotiation may still be necessary to apply the index in unanticipated situations or in the event that the index itself disappears or becomes inappropriate.

4. *Open-Term Provisions.* Because of the difficulties and risks inherent in trying to negotiate arrangements to take place far in the future, some transaction agreements specifically provide that certain matters will be negotiated at a later time, perhaps years after the contract has been signed and the transaction implemented. For example, the electricity company might agree to negotiate appropriate senior management training programs after it has constructed the facility and begun to hire local managers. This type of provision might be called an "open-term" clause because the matter in question has been left open for negotiation at a later time.

In a strict sense, of course, the subsequent negotiation of an open term is not really a *re*negotiation of anything, since the parties have not yet agreed on any elements of that provision. In a broader sense, however, the negotiation of an open term at a later time will have the effect of modifying the overall relationship between the parties. Moreover, it is not inconceivable that one or both of the parties could use the opportunity of negotiating the open term as an occasion to seek concessions or changes in other terms through the common negotiating device of linking issues. For example, the power company might offer a particularly attractive management training program if the government would agree to certain desired regulatory changes.

5. *Renegotiation Clauses.* In an effort to balance the imperatives of contractual stability with flexibility, long-term agreements sometimes contain a definite clause that obligates the parties to renegotiate specified terms affected by changes in circumstances or unforeseen developments, such as those concerning construction costs, governmental regulations, or commodity prices. For example, an oil exploration contract between the government of Qatar and an oil company provided that the two sides would negotiate

future arrangements for the use of natural gas not associated with oil discoveries if commercial quantities of such "non-associated" gas were later found in the contract area.[9] In addition, renegotiation clauses in investment contracts often accompany stabilization clauses by which a host country government promises that any changes in laws or regulations will not adversely affect the foreign investment project. The effect of the two clauses is to obligate the host government and the project company to enter into negotiations to restore the financial equilibrium that such new laws and regulations may have destroyed.

An intra-deal renegotiation clause obligates the parties only to negotiate, not to agree. If the two sides have negotiated in good faith but fail to agree, that failure cannot justify liability on the part of one of the parties. In order to bring finality to the process of intra-deal renegotiation, long-term agreements sometimes include a "contract adaptation clause," which stipulates that on the happening of certain specified events the parties will first seek to negotiate a solution and, failing that, refer their problem to a third party for either a recommendation or a binding decision, depending on the desire of the parties to the contract. Certain institutions, such as the International Chamber of Commerce, have developed rules and facilities to help carry out the contract adaptation process.

Extra-Deal Renegotiation

No deal is forever. And no deal covers everything. Extra-deal renegotiation is a means to enable the parties to cope with the unexpected.

The Context of Extra-Deal Renegotiations

In an extra-deal renegotiation, one party is insisting on renegotiating terms of a valid contract that contains no express provision authorizing renegotiation. Unlike negotiations for the original transaction, which are generally fueled by both sides' hopes for future benefits, extra-deal negotiations begin with both parties' disappointed expectations. One side has failed to achieve the benefits expected from the transaction, and the other is being asked to give up something for which it bargained hard and which it hoped to enjoy for a long time. And whereas both parties to the negotiation of a proposed new venture participate willingly, if not eagerly, one party always participates reluctantly, if not downright unwillingly, in an extra-deal renegotiation.

Beyond mere disappointed expectations, extra-deal renegotiations, by their very nature, can create bad feelings and mistrust. One side believes it is being asked to give up something to which it has a legal and moral right. It views the other side as having gone back on its word, as having acted in bad faith by reneging on the deal. Indeed, the reluctant party may even feel that it's being coerced into participating in extra-deal renegotiations since a refusal to do so would result in losing the investment it has already made in the transaction. In most cases, it is very difficult for the parties to see extra-deal renegotiations as anything more than a process in which one side wins and the other side loses. Whereas the negotiation of any transaction in first instance is usually about the degree to which each side will share in expected benefits, an extra-deal renegotiation is often about allocating a loss. At the same time, because the parties are bound together in a legal and economic relationship, it is usually much harder for one or both of them to walk away from a troubled transaction than it is for two unconnected parties.

In most countries, the law does not oblige a party to enter into renegotiations, no matter how much conditions have changed or how heavy the costs incurred by the other side since the contract was originally made. Indeed, English common law at one time viewed renegotiated contracts under certain conditions as invalid since they lacked the legal requirement of consideration in those cases in which, as a result of renegotiation, a party was promising to do no more than it was already obligated to do under its original contract. In general, a party being asked to renegotiate an existing agreement has a legal right to refuse to renegotiate and to insist on performance in accordance with the letter of the contract. On the other hand, requests or, in some cases, demands for renegotiation of an existing agreement are often accompanied by express or implied threats, including governmental intervention, expropriation, slowdown in performance, or the complete repudiation or cancellation of the contract itself.

In response, of course, a party facing a demand for renegotiation usually has a legal remedy in a court to enforce its contract and will often threaten to assert it. However, its willingness to pursue a legal remedy to its conclusion, rather than renegotiate, will usually depend on its evaluation of that remedy in relation to the results it expects from renegotiation. To the extent that the net benefits (i.e., benefits minus costs) from renegotiation exceed the expected net benefits from litigation, a rational party will ordinarily engage in the requested renegotiation. But if either before or during the renegotiation, a party decides that the net benefits to be derived from litigation will exceed the net benefits to be gained in renegotiation, that party will normally pursue its legal remedies.

On its side, the party asking for renegotiation will be making its own cost/benefit analysis of the relative merits of contract repudiation and its probable fate in litigation. As long as it thinks that the net benefits of repudiating the contract are less than the net benefits of respecting it, the contractual relationship will continue. But when for whatever reason it judges the respective net benefits to be the opposite, the result will be a demand for renegotiation with the threat of eventual repudiation in the background.

A party's reluctance to agree to an extra-deal renegotiation may be due not only to the impact of renegotiation on the contract in question but on other contracts and relationships as well. Renegotiation of a transaction with one particular party may set an undesirable precedent for other renegotiations with other parties. For example, concessions by a civil service union to one government department may lead another department to seek equal treatment by demanding extra-deal renegotiations of its own labor agreements.

The Causes of Extra-Deal Renegotiation

Although the causes of extra-deal renegotiations in individual cases are numerous, they generally fall into one of two basic categories: (1) the parties' imperfect contract with respect to their underlying transaction, or (2) changed circumstances after they have signed their agreement.

The Parties' Imperfect Contract

The goal of any written contract is to express the full meaning of the parties' agreement concerning their proposed transaction. Despite lawyers' belief in their abilities to capture that agreement in lengthy and detailed contracts, in practice a written contract, particularly in long-term arrangements, can only achieve that goal imperfectly, largely for three reasons. First, the parties to long-term agreements are inherently incapable of predicting all of the events and conditions that may affect their transactions in the future because that would require perfect foresight. Second, the transaction costs of making contracts limit the resources that the parties are able to devote to the contracting process, further restricting the ability of the parties to make a contract that perfectly reflects their understanding. Third, even if the parties had the requisite foresight and resources to draft a perfect contract, they have no assurance that a court will interpret their contract exactly as they intended. In many transactions, the problem of accurately negotiating and articulating the parties' intent in a long-term arrangement is particularly difficult because of their differing cultures, business practices, ideologies, political systems, and laws—factors that often impede a true common understanding and inhibit the development of a working relationship.

Changed Circumstances

Changes in circumstances since the time of the original contract are a second major cause for post-deal renegotiations. A sudden fall in commodity prices, the outbreak of civil war, the development of a new technology, or the imposition of currency controls are examples of changes in circumstance that often force the parties back to the negotiating table. As Raymond Vernon argued over three decades ago with respect to foreign investment projects with governments, a bargain once struck will inevitably become obsolete for one of the parties and issues once agreed upon will be reopened at a later time. Long-term agreements with governments, in Vernon's words, are "obsolescing bargains."[10]

Generally speaking, changes in circumstances can either increase or decrease the costs and benefits of the agreement to the parties. When a change in circumstances means that the cost of respecting a contract for one of the parties is greater than the cost of abandoning it, the result is usually rejection of the deal or a demand for its renegotiation. The notions of "costs" and "benefits" are not limited to purely economic calculations. Political and social costs and benefits must also be accounted for. For example, in the case involving an investment project to build a luxury resort near the Giza pyramids in Egypt, the Egyptian government originally signed the agreement because it believed the economic benefits of the project would exceed its potential costs. But when public and international opposition became strong and persistent, the government cancelled the project because it judged the political costs to outweigh its potential economic benefits.

A Case of Extra-Deal Renegotiation: The Dabhol Power Project

We can gain an understanding of the dynamics at work in extra-deal renegotiations by examining a specific case, the renegotiations involved in the Dabhol Power project in India, an incident that received significant media attention in 1995–1996.

Background

In the early 1990s, India, suffering a chronic shortage of electricity that was impeding its development, began actively to attract foreign investors to its power sector. In response to these government overtures, Enron, then a Houston-based energy company, along with General Electric and the Bechtel Corporation, developed a project to build a $2 billion electrical generating station in the town of Dabhol, 120 miles south of Mumbai, in the State of Maharashtra. A key element of the project was an agreement that the Maharashtra State Electricity Board (MSEB), a public utility, would purchase all the power produced by the Dabhol project for a period of twenty years. At the time of the agreement, the Maharashtra state government was then under the control of India's Congress Party, which also controlled the Indian central government. For many observers, the project looked like a win-win deal for both sides: it would help India solve its power shortage problem and would provide the investors with a good rate of return while allowing them to enter a potentially huge energy market.

The Forces for Change

Once the deal was signed, both Enron and the Indian central and state governments were surprised by the growing public opposition to the Dabhol power project as construction activity proceeded. Indian activists and organizations filed lawsuits in the Bombay High Court, challenging the legality of the project and the processes by which it was negotiated. Although the court dismissed the complaints, political opposition continued to mount. Specifically, the political opposition alliance of the Bharatiya Janata Party (BJP) and the Shiva Sena took up the issue on the floor of the Maharashtra State Assembly. As they prepared for state elections scheduled for March 1995, they made opposition to the Dabhol project and the power purchase agreement a centerpiece in their campaign. Emphasizing Hindu nationalism and warning against the dangers of American economic and cultural imperialism, BJP–Shiv Sena politicians encouraged public opposition to the project in their campaign rhetoric. They charged that the Dabhol project was offering India nothing that India could not do for itself, that the power tariff was exorbitant and would hurt the poor, that the rate of return was exploitative, and that the whole negotiation process had been tainted by corruption.

In the state assembly elections of March 1995, the BJP–Shiv Sena alliance won a majority of seats and thereby ousted from government the incumbent Congress Party. In May, the new government appointed a cabinet subcommittee to investigate the Dabhol project. The committee submitted a report in July recommending that the state repudiate Phase I of the project and cancel Phase

II. The committee based its recommendation on several grounds, including the absence of transparency in the negotiation process, the lack of competitive bidding procedure, the relaxation by the previous government of certain regulations relating to the project, the great expense of the project, the high electricity tariff rate and its continuing escalation, the obligation of the MSEB to pay for electricity whether or not it was actually used, and the failure of the project negotiations to address environmental concerns.

On the basis of this report, the state government, under its new Chief Minister, and the MSEB formally canceled the power purchase agreement with the Dabhol Power Company. At this point in its development, the Dabhol project had incurred sunk costs of approximately $300 million, and each day of delay on construction was estimated to cost an additional $250,000.

In response, the Dabhol Power Company and the project sponsors invoked their legal rights under the power purchase agreement by instituting arbitration in London against the MSEB and the Maharashtra state government, claiming damages in excess of $300 million. The State of Maharashtra reacted by bringing suit in the Bombay High Court to invalidate the arbitration clause and the guarantee of MSEB payments on the grounds that both had been secured through illegal means. The U.S. government issued a statement critical of the contract repudiation, asserting that it would have negative consequences for foreign investment in India. Foreign investors considering India became demonstrably more cautious and expressed their concern over the incident. The Indian press appeared to be divided over the wisdom of Maharashtra's action. In the face of this growing controversy, Deputy Chief Minister Munde, who had chaired the Dabhol project review committee, stated: "Our decision is firm. We do not wish to renegotiate."

Renegotiating the Dabhol Project

While pursuing arbitration, Enron and its partners made it clear to the Maharashtra authorities that they would be willing to renegotiate the power purchase agreement. In the fall of 1995, discussions to revive the project took place between Enron executives and Maharashtra officials and political leaders. Shortly thereafter, the Chief Minister announced that Maharashtra state would undertake a review of the project and promised to reopen negotiations in November. To carry out the review and renegotiation, he appointed a panel consisting of the president of the MSEB, the power secretary of Maharashtra State, and four other academic and industry experts, in contrast to the first review panel that had consisted solely of government ministers.

For two weeks, the review panel not only met with Enron to discuss proposals for restructuring the Dabhol project, but it also listened to principal critics of the project. The key issues in the discussions with Enron concerned the electricity tariff, capital costs, payment terms, and the environment. Finally, on November 19, 1995, the panel submitted a proposal to the Maharashtra state government outlining the renegotiated terms of the Dabhol project to which the panel and the investors had agreed. On January 8, 1996, after some delay, the Maharashtra government agreed to accept the panel proposal for renegotiated terms, which eventually became the basis for amending the power purchase agreement between the Dabhol Power Company, the state of Maharashtra, and the MSEB, an event that took place on February 23, 1996. Key elements in the renegotiated power purchase agreement were a reduction in the electricity tariff, an increase in the power plant's generation capacity, and measures to protect the environment and the local population from the plant's operations.[11]

Both the investors and the state of Maharashtra claimed the renegotiation as a victory. The renegotiation process dealt with the political imperatives driving the government at a price that the project partners were willing to pay. The Dabhol plant was completed and began producing power in 1999, but in 2001 it was closed down when the MSEB failed to pay an electricity bill of $45 million. This time extra-deal renegotiations did not solve the problem.

Some Principles to Guide Extra-Deal Renegotiations

Since the risk of extra-deal project renegotiations is always present in any agreement, negotiators should ask themselves two basic questions:

1. How can the likelihood of extra-deal renegotiations be reduced?
2. When renegotiations actually occur, how should the parties conduct them to make the process as productive and fair as possible?

In answering these questions, you need to distinguish actions you should take before and after the transaction has broken down and one party is demanding renegotiation or threatening to reject the deal entirely. Thus in the case of the Dabhol project, we need to consider the actions that investors might have taken to avoid the conflict and renegotiation that actually took place, as well as the actions that it took when faced with the cancellation of the power purchase agreement.

Before Deal Breakdown

How can the parties to a contract lessen the likelihood that one of the parties will demand renegotiation during the term of the contract?

Guideline #1: Work to create a relationship between the parties and recognize that a signed contract does not necessarily create a relationship. For a long-term transaction to be stable and productive for both sides, it must be founded on a relationship, a complex set of interactions characterized by cooperation and a minimal degree of trust. A relationship also implies a connection between the parties. It is the existence of a solid relationship between the parties to a transaction that allows them to face unforeseen circumstances and hardships in a productive and creative manner. A contract, no matter how detailed and lengthy, does not create a business relationship. Just as a map is not a country, but only an imperfect description thereof, a contract is not a business relationship, but only an imperfect sketch of what the relationship should be. A contract may be a necessary condition for certain kinds of relationships, but it is usually not a sufficient condition. While negotiators must be concerned about the adequacy of contractual provisions, they should also seek to determine that a solid foundation for a relationship is in place. Accordingly, a negotiator should also ask a variety of non-contractual questions during the negotiating process: How well do the parties know one another? What mechanisms are in place to foster communications between the two sides after the contract is signed? To what extent are there genuine links and connections between the parties to the agreement? Is the deal balanced and advantageous for both sides?

Regardless of culture, when one party fails to respect its contractual obligations to another party, the existence of a valuable relationship between the parties is more likely to facilitate a negotiated resolution of their dispute than if no such relationship exists. The reason for this phenomenon is that the aggrieved party probably views the relationship with the offending party as more valuable than the individual claim arising out of the failure to honor the contractual provision. Thus in a workout, a bank is often willing to renegotiate a loan with a delinquent debtor company or country when the bank considers that the prospect of future business with the debtor is likely. Bondholders of the same debtor, on the other hand, will generally be more resistant to renegotiation than banks since bondholders generally do not have the same opportunity for a profitable business relationship in the future.

In reviewing the Dabhol Power project case, we can conclude that although the parties had negotiated a detailed contract to govern their deal, no real business relationship appears to have existed at all between Enron, the MSEB, and the various concerned Indian government departments. Specifically, at the time the Power Purchase Agreement was signed, there was no real connection between Enron and India itself. No Indian party was asked to participate in any meaningful way in the development and management of the Dabhol Power Company. The Indian public had little knowledge of Enron or of the proposed Dabhol project, which was negotiated largely in secrecy. The only role for any Indian entity was to buy electricity according to the Power Purchase Agreement. The negotiation of the contract had been contentious, and Enron appeared to have little appreciation of Indian concerns about foreign investment in general and the Dabhol Power project in particular. Finally, Enron and India seemed to know relatively little about one another, a particularly egregious oversight given the size and importance of the project. Thus, after nearly eighteen months of negotiation, investors emerged with a contract but no real business relationship. It had established no basis for cooperation and trust with either the Maharashtra State Electricity Board, the Maharashtra State Government, or the Indian public.

Had Enron and its partners thought in terms of relationship building and acted accordingly, it might have avoided the cancellation of the contract. Involving the Maharashtra State Electricity Board as a partner in the project from the very start of the project might have been a crucial step in building an effective business relationship between Enron and India. Moreover, given India's historical ambivalence toward foreign investment, it was essential that a deal of the magnitude of the Dabhol project be and *appear* balanced and fair to both sides. The project's high rate of return and high power tariff raised important questions in the minds of the Indian public, something that Enron should have sought to address.

Guideline #2: Building a relationship takes time, so don't rush initial negotiations. Negotiators who are concerned to lay the foundation for a relationship as well as to conclude a contract know that sufficient time is required to achieve this goal. While speed of negotiation may appeal to Americans as "efficient" and a recognition of the fact that "time is money," for other cultures a quick negotiation of a complicated transaction may imply overreaching by one of the parties, insufficient consideration of the public interest, or even corruption. Negotiations done in haste invite renegotiation later on. For example, the fact that Enron negotiated a memorandum of understanding with the government of Maharashtra State to build a $2 billion power plant after just three days of discussions during Enron's first visit made the subsequent power purchase agreement vulnerable to challenges from many quarters.

Guideline #3: Provide for intra-deal renegotiations in appropriate transactions. If the risk of change and uncertainty is constant in long-term agreements, how should negotiators cope with it? The traditional method is to write detailed contracts that seek to foresee all possible eventualities. Most modern contracts deny the possibility of change. They therefore rarely provide for adjustments to meet changing circumstances. This assumption of contractual stability has proven false time and time again.

As suggested above, rather than view a long-term transaction as frozen in the detailed provisions of a lengthy contract, it may be more realistic to think of a long-term agreement as a *continuing negotiation* between the parties as they seek to adjust their relationship to the rapidly changing environment in which they must work together. Accordingly, the parties should consider providing in their contract that at specified times or on the happening of specified events, they will renegotiate or at least review certain of the contract's provisions. In this approach, the parties deal with the problem of renegotiation before, rather than after, they sign their contract. Both sides recognize at the outset that the risk of changed circumstances is high in any long-term relationship and that at sometime in the future either side may seek to renegotiate or adjust the contract accordingly. Rather than dismiss the possibility of renegotiation and then be forced to review the entire contract at a later time in an atmosphere of hostility between the partners, it may be better to recognize the possibility of renegotiation at the outset and set down a clear framework to conduct the process.

Guideline #4: Consider a role for mediation or conciliation in the deal. A third party can often help the two sides with their negotiations and renegotiations. Third parties, whether called mediators, conciliators, or advisors, can assist in building and preserving business relations and in resolving disputes without resort to litigation. Consequently, negotiators should consider the possibility of building into their transactions a role for some form of mediation. For example, the contract might provide that before a party can resort to litigation to settle a dispute, it must use the services of a mediator or conciliator for a specific period of time in an attempt to negotiate a settlement of the conflict.

After Deal Breakdown

When one side has repudiated or demanded renegotiation of the basic contract governing their relationship, how should one or both of the parties proceed?

Guideline #1: Resist the temptation to make belligerent or moralistic responses to a demand for renegotiation but seek to understand the basis of the demand. A party facing a demand for extra-deal renegotiations often counters it with hostile, belligerent, or moralistic objections. Such responses are hardly ever effective in persuading the other side to end its insistence on renegotiation since that party has already determined that its own vital interests require repudiation or renegotiation of the agreement. Normally, it is only by dealing with those interests that the two sides in a renegotiation can resolve the conflict. Moreover, like the Indian opposition in the Dabhol case, the party asking for renegotiation almost always asserts equally moralistic arguments to justify its own demands: the contract is exploitative, the negotiators were corrupt, one side used duress, the other side was ignorant of all the underlying factors, or the basic circumstances of the deal have changed in a fundamental way.

While respect for agreements is indeed a norm in virtually all societies and may even rise to the level of a universal principle of law, most cultures also provide relief, in varying degrees, from the binding force of a contract in a variety of circumstances. "A deal is a deal," a principle embodied in the Latin phrase *pacta sunt servanda*, is certainly an expression of a fundamental rule of human relations, but so is the statement "things have changed," captured in another Latin expression, *rebus sic stantibus*. While a request for extra-deal renegotiations may provoke bad feelings in one party, an outright refusal to renegotiate may also create ill will on the other side, which will see it as an attempt to perpetuate an unjust bargain.

One may also argue that in many transactions, particularly between parties from different cultures, there are in effect two agreements: the legal contract, which sets out enforceable rights and duties; and their "foundation relationship," which reflects their fundamental understanding in all its dimensions, legal and nonlegal. An important, implied aspect of this relationship is an understanding, given the impossibility of predicting all future contingencies, that if problems develop in the future the two sides will engage in negotiations to adjust their relationship in a mutually beneficial way.

Guideline #2: The party facing a demand for renegotiation should evaluate the worth of the claim for breach of contract against the value of a continuing relationship. The extent of a party's willingness to renegotiate an agreement will usually be in direct proportion to the value it attaches to its potential future relationship with the other side. If it judges that relationship to be worth more than its claim for breach of contract, it will ordinarily be willing to engage in extra-deal renegotiation. If, on the other hand, it concludes that its claim is worth more than the benefits from a continuing relationship, it will usually insist on its contractual rights to the point of using litigation to protect them. For example, one of the factors that encouraged the investors to renegotiate with the Maharashtra government after the cancellation of its electricity supply contract was the prospect of undertaking numerous energy projects throughout India in the years ahead. Enron and its partners clearly judged those potential relationships to be worth more than winning an arbitration award in a case that would certainly be a long protracted struggle. They therefore constantly remained open to renegotiation throughout its conflict with the state of Maharashtra.

Often an aggrieved party facing a demand for renegotiation cannot accurately evaluate the worth of its claim or the value of a renegotiated contract without first engaging some kind of discussions with the other side. Moreover, satisfaction of its claim through litigation against the other side is almost always subject to long delays, a further inducement to enter into renegotiations. Indeed, one of the functions of the delays inherent in pursuing legal remedies is to give the parties an opportunity to negotiate an efficient solution to their conflict.

Guideline #3: Look for ways to create value in the renegotiation. A party facing a demand for renegotiation has a tendency to see the process as the worst kind of win/lose activity, one in which any advantage gained by the other side is an automatic loss to itself. As a result, an unwilling participant in an extra-deal renegotiation tends to be intransigent, to quibble over the smallest issues, to voice recriminations, and generally to fight a rearguard action throughout the process. By pursuing this approach, the parties may fail to capture the maximum gains possible from their encounter. Joint problem-solving negotiation and integrative bargaining are as applicable to an extra-deal renegotiation as they are to the negotiation of the deal in first instance. The challenge for both sides in a renegotiation is to create an atmosphere in which problem solving can readily take place. Even if a party feels forced into an extra-deal renegotiation, it should approach the process as an opportunity to secure gains from the process by raising other issues. Thus in the renegotiations between the investors and the Maharashtra State government over their electricity supply contract, although Maharashtra State gained a reduced power tariff, the investors secured the right to increase the capacity of their power plant.

Guideline #4: The parties should fully understand the alternatives to succeeding in the renegotiation—especially their costs. The alternative to a successful extra-deal renegotiation in most cases is litigation in which the party seeking renegotiation will be the defendant and the party refusing it is the plaintiff. Litigation has risks and costs for both sides, and it is important that both sides understand them thoroughly as they approach the renegotiation process so they can accurately evaluate the worth of any proposal put forward.

Often the party demanding renegotiation has a tendency to undervalue the risks and costs of litigation while the party facing that demand tends to overvalue its benefits. It is therefore important for each side as part of its negotiating strategy to be sure that the other has a realistic evaluation of its alternatives to a renegotiated agreement. Sometimes an aggrieved party may try to focus the other's attention on those costs by commencing a lawsuit while the renegotiation discussions are in progress. In the Dabhol case, at the time the Maharashtra government cancelled the electricity supply agreement, it probably assumed that its action would entail relatively little cost. It also seemed to have assumed that other investors would be willing to step into the shoes vacated by Enron and its partners or that it would be able to find indigenous solutions to the state's power shortage. Once those assumptions proved false and once the investors had begun an arbitration case in London with a claim of $300 million, the state of Maharashtra, with a renewed appreciation of the costs of outright contract cancellation, became considerably more open to renegotiation than it was at the time it cancelled the contract.

Guideline #5: Involve either directly or indirectly all necessary parties in the renegotiation. A successful renegotiation may not only require the participation of the parties who signed the original agreement, but it may also necessitate the involvement of other parties who did not sign it but who gained an interest in the transaction afterwards. Such secondary parties may include labor unions, creditors, suppliers, governmental departments, and in the case of diplomatic negotiations, other sovereign states. For example, in the renegotiation of a loan between a bank and a troubled real estate developer with a partially completed office building, no new agreement can be reached without the participation, directly or indirectly, of the unpaid construction contractor whose lien on the property can block refinancing of the project. It is therefore important in organizing any renegotiation to determine all the parties, both primary and secondary, that should participate and then to decide whether they should be involved in the face-to-face renegotiations between the primary parties or dealt with in separate discussions.

Guideline #6: Design the right forum and process for the renegotiation. Both sides should think hard about the appropriate process for launching and conducting extra-deal renegotiations. Renegotiations often emerge out of a crisis characterized by severe conflict, threats, and high emotion. An appropriate process for the renegotiation may help to mollify the parties and reduce the negative consequences of the crisis on their subsequent discussions. An inappropriate process, on the other hand, may serve to heighten those negative consequences and impede the renegotiations. The government of the Maharashtra, after receiving the recommendation of a cabinet subcommittee, cancelled the contract with Enron and also declared publicly that it would not renegotiate the agreement. In that context, if renegotiations were ever to take place, the parties would need to create a process that would preserve the government's dignity and prestige. Ultimately, the government chose to appoint a "Review Panel" consisting of energy experts to reexamine the project. The Panel met with Enron representatives, as well as project critics, and then submitted a proposal to the government, containing the terms of a renegotiated electricity supply agreement to which Enron had agreed. The use of a Review Panel of experts to conduct what amounted to a renegotiation, rather than face-to-face discussions between government and Enron, served to protect governmental dignity. Moreover, the Panel's status as a group of independent experts, rather than politicians, tended to give its recommendations the legitimacy needed to persuade the public that the renegotiated agreement protected Indian interests.

In some cases, the way in which the parties frame the renegotiation may influence its success. For example, rather than use the label "renegotiation," a term that conjures up negative implications of fundamental changes in the sanctity of contract, the parties may refer to the process as a "review," " restructuring," "rescheduling," positioning the process as an effort to clarify ambiguities in the existing agreement, rather than to change basic principles. This approach, at least formally, respects the sanctity of contract and thereby may avoid some of the friction and hostility engendered by demanding outright extra-deal renegotiations. "Waiver" is yet another way of framing a renegotiation, an approach that respects the agreement yet enables the burdened party to obtain relief from certain contractual obligations.

Guideline #7: Consider a role for a mediator in the renegotiation process. In the stress and hostility often engendered by an extra-deal renegotiation, a mediator or other neutral third person may be able to aid the parties to overcome the obstacles between them so as to reach a satisfactory renegotiated agreement. A mediator may make a positive contribution to the process by helping design and manage the renegotiation process so that the parties will have the maximum opportunities to create value through their interaction, by assisting with the communications between the two sides in a way that will facilitate positive results from their interactions, and by suggesting substantive solutions to the problems that the parties encounter during the course of their extra-deal renegotiation.

Conclusion: Four Rules for Renegotiation

Many persons view a contract renegotiation in negative terms. For them, it is an aberration, a disreputable practice that evokes images of broken promises, disappointed expectations, and bargains made but not kept. From the viewpoint of anyone facing demands for an unwanted renegotiation, such a reaction is normal and understandable. But from the vantage of society, renegotiation plays a constructive role in human relations at all levels. If Karl Llewellyn is correct that the work of agreements in society is a struggle of life against form, the function of renegotiation in the social order is to mediate that struggle, to allow life and form to adjust to one another over the long term at least cost.

As you contemplate the challenge of renegotiation in your dealing with governments, bear in mind the following rules:

Rule #1: The risk of renegotiation is present in any transaction but it is a particular risk in transactions with governments, primarily because of the political pressures and imperatives affecting government actions.

Rule #2: As a result, incorporate into your negotiation strategies tactics and mechanisms to deal with this risk.

Rule #3: Distinguish among the three types of renegotiation—post-deal, intra-deal, and extra deal—and apply the relevant principles outline above for each.

Rule #4: Develop strategies that reduce the likelihood of renegotiation, as well as strategies that enable renegotiation, if and when it occurs, to proceed productively at least cost.

• CHAPTER NINE •

On the Manner of Negotiating with Governments: Some Final Advice

> "And yet I may hazard a guess that there is perhaps no employment in all his Majesty's service more difficult to discharge than that of negotiation."
>
> —FRANÇOIS DE CALLIÈRES

Nearly three hundred years ago, François de Callières, a distinguished French diplomat, wrote one of the first practical manuals on negotiating with governments in a book entitled *De la manière de négocier avec les souverains,* translated into English as *On the Manner of Negotiating with Princes.*[1] Originally published in 1716, the book is still considered a model introduction to the subject. While de Callières's language may sound quaint to us today and while his fundamental concern was with the use of negotiation in diplomacy between states in the eighteenth century, its pages contain much useful advice for negotiators who must deal with governments today. Although you may think of yourself as a hard-nosed dealmaker in your negotiations with other companies, you may be more effective in negotiating with governments if you see yourself and behave as a diplomat.

Ten Rules of Diplomacy

Based on de Callières's thoughts, the following ten simple rules are offered to guide you in your own dealings with local, state, national, or foreign governments. They are precisely the principles developed earlier in this book.

Rule #1: Recognize the Necessity of Continual Negotiation

De Callières stressed "the necessity of continual negotiation"[2] between states through their permanent representatives as the basis of modern diplomacy—a novel idea in its time but one that modern diplomats take for granted today. Twenty-first century negotiators must also recognize, as this book has argued, that a productive relationship with a government involves a constant process of negotiation. Just as negotiations do not stop when two countries seal a treaty, negotiations do not end when your company signs a contract with a government department or agency. Develop your business strategies and deploy your resources with that principle constantly in mind.

Rule #2: Study and Saturate Your Mind

Prepare thoroughly for every negotiation. You should not only understand the substance of the transaction, you should exhaustively research the organizations, politics, cultures, and individuals involved in the negotiation. De Callières's constant and repeated message to negotiators is "to study" before undertaking negotiations. His list of matters to study includes virtually every dimension of the country and the people with whom the negotiator will come into contact. Recognizing that all negotiators are agents, he also advises a negotiator to "saturate his mind with the thoughts of his master."[3] Negotiators with governments in the twenty-first century need to prepare no less, as Chapter 3 and other sections of this book have emphasized.

Rule #3: Be an Apt Listener

People often think that negotiation is mostly about talking and that the best negotiators are the best talkers. That view misconceives the nature of the negotiation process. In the words of de Callières, "one of the most necessary qualities in a good negotiator is to be an apt listener," and, "in order to succeed in this kind of work one must rather listen than speak."[4]

More generally, successful negotiation requires keen perception of yourself as well as of the other side. As we have seen, the ability to understand interests and to overcome barriers to agreement with a government depends first and foremost on your perceptive powers. As you sit at the negotiating table, you are like a director in a television studio watching three TV monitors showing the images taken by three different cameras from three different angles of the same set. The negotiator's three cameras are focused on (1) the words and actions of the other side; (2) your own words and actions; and (3) the effect of your words and actions on the other side. Like the television director, a negotiator must constantly process information from each of the monitors and then make a decision about the next steps.

Rule #4: Know and Stay Faithful to Your Goal

An important step in preparation is to carefully determine what you want from a deal before you start negotiations. You need to identify in advance precisely at what point an agreement is not in your interest compared to other options and be careful not to change objectives in the heat of negotiations. On this issue, negotiators should heed de Callières's advice, "The lack of firmness of which I speak here is a common fault of those who have a lively imagination for every kind of accident which may befall, and hinders them from determining with vigor and dispatch the means by which action should be taken. They will look at a matter on so many sides that they forget in which direction they are traveling."[5]

Rule #5: Have a Mind Fertile in Expedients

While you should know your bottom line, you should also realize that there are many ways to arrive at it. Earlier chapters have stressed the need for creativity and flexibility in shaping agreements. Remain open to new approaches and search for novel solutions to allow both sides to advance their interests. Again, in the words of de Callières, "[A negotiator] must also have a mind so fertile in expedients as easily to smooth away the difficulties which he meets in the course of his duty . . ."[6]

Rule #6: Have the Patience of a Clockmaker

Negotiating agreements with governments and then managing them through unexpected difficulties is a time-consuming process, one that invariably takes longer than you originally planned. If you are not prepared to commit the time, don't get into the negotiation. Shortcuts usually fail. Establish deadlines with care and avoid ultimatums. De Callières's advice of three hundred years ago is valid today for negotiators encountering difficulties in their negotiations, given governments' tendency to delay: "Indeed, he must behave as a good clockmaker would when his clock has gone out of order; he must labor to remove the difficulty, or at all events to circumvent its results."[7] A negotiator needs "a patience which no trial can break down."[8]

Rule #7: Be Master of Yourself and Avoid the Choleric Word

Never become emotional at the negotiating table. Emotions cloud judgment and interfere with perception. Equally important, different cultures interpret displays of emotion differently. An angry statement that might be tolerated in negotiations in the United States may be taken as evidence of insanity in Thailand. In such a setting, your outburst may entirely destroy your credibility with the other side, as de Callières recognized when he stressed the need for a negotiator to be "master of himself," for ". . . a choleric word may poison the minds of those with whom negotiations are in process."[9]

In short, keep your cool.

Rule #8: Show Respect

Negotiations with governments, as we have seen, bring you into contact with a wide variety of personalities, a diversity of cultures and situations, and the many special forms and protocols of states and their subdivisions. Approach each one with a respect and willingness to learn. Negotiation is fundamentally a learning process. One of the marks of inexperienced negotiators is the attitude that they have little to learn from the other side. That attitude is not only perceived as arrogance by the other side, but it also prevents executives from getting the information they need to make a good deal. De Callières counseled negotiators to "reveal an innate respect for the person whom they are addressing," and "to show genuine and sincere interest in the welfare of his new associates and in all the customs of the court and the habits of the people." A negotiator quickly discovers that "it is easy to single out the good points, and that there is not profit to be had in denouncing the bad ones, for the very good reason that nothing the diplomatist can say or do will alter the domestic habits or laws of the country . . ."[10] That remains good advice today.

Rule #9: Search Constantly for the Needs and Interests of Others

This book has stressed the importance of understanding interests, both yours and the other side's, in negotiating with governments. Throughout his manual, de Callières also emphasized the key role that interests, both the public interests of governments and the private interests of negotiators, play in diplomacy. "The secret of negotiation is to harmonize the interests of the parties concerned."[11] To understand interests, negotiators must put themselves in the position of others. "The more often he thus puts himself in the position of others, the more subtle and effective will his arguments be."[12] "He should therefore at the outset think rather of what is in their minds than of immediately expressing what is in his own."[13]

Rule #10: Accentuate the Positive

Throughout your discussions with the other side, emphasize the positive aspects of the transaction and the relationships you are trying to forge. Stress the points of agreement with your counterparts and the progress you are making in the talks. Try to make negative points in a positive way. For de Callières, "the great secret of negotiation is to bring out prominently the common advantage to both parties of any proposal and so to link those advantages that they may appear equally balanced to both parties."[14]

❖ ❖ ❖ ❖ ❖ ❖

Keep in mind these ten rules of diplomacy as you go about the task of negotiating with governments. They have successfully guided relationships among nations over the last three hundred years. They will also help you in making and managing relationships with governments today.

Notes

Chapter 1

1. Miriam D. Silverman, *Stopping the Plant; The St. Lawrence Cement Controversy and the Battle for Quality of Life in the Hudson Valley* (Albany, N.Y.: SUNY Press, 2006), p. 9.
2. See *The Medicare Drug War: An Army of 1000 Lobbyists Pushes a Medicare Law that Puts Drug Company and HMO Profits Ahead of Patients and Taxpayers* (Public Citizen Report: Congress Watch, 2004).
3. *Minnesota State Board For Community Colleges v. Knight* 104 S. Ct. 1058 (1984).
4. See Daniel P. Selmi, "The Promise and Limits of Negotiated Rulemaking: Evaluating the Negotiation of a Regional Air Quality Rule," 35 *Environmental Law* (2005), p. 415.
5. Diane Valden, "Wilzig Launches Suit Over Track," *The Independent*, February 2, 2007, p. 1.
6. CBS News, "Cashing in For Profit," January 5, 2005. See also, Renae Merle, "Long Fall for Pentagon Star," *Washington Post*, November 14, 2004, p. A01.
7. See www.transparency.org.
8. Robert Klitgaard, *Controlling Corruption* (Berkeley: University of California Press, 1988), p. 75.
9. Quoted in Joseph Q. Wilson, *Bureaucracy: What Governments Do and Why They Do It* (New York: Basic Books, 2000), p. 197.

Chapter 2

1. Address to the White House Conference on Small Business, April 15, 1986.

2. Jane Alexander, *Command Performance: An Actress in the Theater of Politics* (New York: Public Affairs, 2000), p. 57.
3. Gardiner Harris, "A Hard-Learned Lesson on Dealing with U.S. Regulators," *The New York Times,* February 3, 2006, p. C4.
4. Quoted in *The New York Times,* November 3, 1986.
5. See Jeswald W. Salacuse, *The Global Negotiator: Making, Managing, and Mending Deals Around the World in the Twenty-first Century* (New York: Palgrave Macmillan, 2003), p. 99.
6. Jack Welch and John A. Byrne, *Jack: Straight From the Gut* (New York: Warner Books, 2001), p. 366.
7. Author's interview with the late Charles Francis Adams, former chairman of Raytheon.
8. David Lax and James Sebenius, *The Manager as Negotiator: Bargaining for Cooperation and Competitive Gain* (New York: Free Press, 1986), pp. 354–355.
9. Miriam D. Silverman, *Stopping the Plant: The St Lawrence Cement Controversy and the Battle for Quality of Life in the Hudson Valley* (Albany, N.Y.: SUNY Press, 2006), p. 110.
10. James Q. Wilson, *Bureaucracy: What Government Agencies Do and Why They Do It* (New York: Basic Books, 2000), pp. 115 et seq.
11. Ibid., p. 222.

Chapter 3

1. For a discussion of the process of giving advice, see Jeswald W. Salacuse, *The Wise Advisor: What Every Professional Should Know About Consulting and Counseling* (Westport, Conn.: Praeger, 2000).
2. Roger W. Fisher, William Ury, and Bruce Patton, *Getting to YES: Negotiating Agreement Without Giving In, 2nd Edition* (New York: Penguin, 1991).
3. See Bill Vlasic and Bradley A. Stertz, *Taken for a Ride: How Daimler-Benz Drove Off with Chrysler* (New York: William Morrow, 2000).
4. Edmund L. Andrews, "AOL–Time Warner Merger is Cleared by the Europeans," *New York Times,* October 12, 2000, p. C4.
5. Akilagpa Sawyer, "Redoing An Old Deal: Case Study of the Renegotiation of the Valco Agreement" (unpublished paper, 1991). See also Fui S. Tsikata, ed., *Essays from the Ghana-Valco Renegotiations: 1982–85* (Accra: Ghana Publishing, 1986).
6. For a discussion of this tripartite analysis within the context of dip-

lomatic negotiations, see I. William Zartman and Maureen R. Berman, *The Practical Negotiator* (New Haven, Conn.: Yale University Press, 1982).

Chapter 4

1. Carol J. Loomis, "Warren Buffett's Wild Ride at Salomon: A Harrowing Bizarre Tale of Misdeeds and Mistakes that Pushed Salomon to the Brink and Produced the 'Most Important Day' in Warren Buffett's Life," *Fortune*, October 27, 1997, p. 114.
2. Harvard Business School, *Salomon Brothers* (HBS case study, no. 9-305-019, rev. May 5, 2005). See also Carol J. Loomis, op. cit.
3. James Q. Wilson, *Bureaucracy: What Governments Do and Why They Do It* (New York: Basic Books, 2000).
4. See, e.g., Michel Crozier, *The Bureaucratic Phenomenon* (Chicago: University of Chicago Press, 1964).
5. Jonathan Weisman and Bradley Graham, "Dubai Firm to Sell U.S. Port Operations," *Washington Post*, March 10, 2006, p. A01.
6. Gerald R. Ford, *A Time to Heal* (New York: Harper & Row/Reader's Digest, 1979).
7. Miriam D. Silverman, *Stopping the Plant: The St Lawrence Cement Controversy and the Battle for Quality of Life in the Hudson Valley* (Albany, N.Y.: SUNY Press, 2006), p. 110.
8. David McKean, *Tommy the Cork—Washington's Ultimate Insider from Roosevelt to Reagan* (Hanover, N.H.: Steerforth, 2003).
9. Jane Alexander, *Command Performance: An Actress in the Theater of Politics* (New York: Public Affairs, 2000), p. 97.

Chapter 5

1. François de Callières, *On the Manner of Negotiating with Princes*, trans. A. F. Whyte, with an introduction by Charles Handy (New York: Houghton Mifflin, 2000).

———, *De La Manière de négocier avec les souverains. De l'utilité des négociations, du choix des ambassadeurs et des envoyés et des qualitiés nécessaires pour réussir dans ces emplois* (Amsterdam: Pour la Compagnie, 1716). The book has been published in many languages since it was written. The most recent English language version is Francois de Callières, *On the Manner of Negotiating with Princes*, trans. A. F. Whyte, with introduction by Charles Handy,

(New York: Houghton Mifflin, 2000.) A recent French version with a useful bibliography is Francois de Callières, *De La Manière de négocier avec les souverains*, ed. Alain Pekar Lempereur (Paris-Cergy: Essec Irene, 2001).

2. James Q. Wilson, *Bureaucracy: What Governments Do and Why They Do It* (New York: Basic Books, 2000), pp. 300–301.

3. For a full discussion of this case, see Jeswald W. Salacuse, *The Global Negotiator: Making, Managing, and Mending Deals Around the World in the Twenty-First Century* (New York: Palgrave Macmillan), pp. 236–247.

4. Lawrence Susskind, "Negotiating with the Regulators," 8 *Negotiation* (November 2005), pp. 7–9.

5. David McKean, *Tommy the Cork: Washington's Ultimate Insider from Roosevelt to Reagan* (Hanover, N.H.: Steerforth, 2003), p. 197.

6. Harvard Business School, *Salomon Brothers* (HBS case study, no. 9-305-019, rev. May 5, 2005), p. 2.

7. Thomas L. O'Brien, and Landon Thomas, Jr., "It's Cleanup Time at Citi," *New York Times,* November 7, 2004, Section 3, p. 1.

8. François de Callières, *On the Manner of Negotiating with Princes.*

Chapter 6

1. François de Callières, *On the Manner of Negotiating with Princes*, trans. A. F. Whyte, with an introduction by Charles Handy (New York: Houghton Mifflin, 2000), p. 77.

2. Bruce C. Wolpe and Bertram J. Levine, *Lobbying Congress: How the System Works* (Washington, D.C.: Congressional Quarterly Press, 2nd ed., 1996), pp. 29–32.

3. Lawrence Susskind, "Negotiating with the Regulators," 8 *Negotiation* (November 2005), pp. 7–9.

4. Edward T. Hall, *The Silent Language* (Garden City, N.Y.: Doubleday, 1959).

5. C. P. Snow, *The Two Cultures and the Scientific Revolution* (Cambridge, U.K.: Cambridge University Press, 1962).

6. Jeswald W. Salacuse, "Implications for Practitioners," in *Culture and Negotiation*, eds., G.O. Faure and J.Z. Rubin (Newbury Park, Calif.: Sage Publications, 1993), p. 206.

7. George Shultz, *Turmoil and Triumph: My Years as Secretary of State* (New York: Charles Scribner's Sons, 1993), p. 763.

Chapter 7

1. Benjamin C. Esty, *The Chad-Cameroon Petroleum Development and Pipeline Project* (Harvard Business School case N9–202–010, January 17, 2002).
2. See, e.g., Jeffrey Z. Rubin, "International Mediation in Context," in Bercovitch and Rubin, eds. *Mediation in International Relations: Multiple Approaches to Conflict Management* (New York: St. Martin's Press, 1992), pp. 254–565.
3. Quoted in David McKean, *Tommy the Cork—Washington's Ultimate Insider from Roosevelt to Reagan* (Hanover, N.H.: Steerforth, 2003), p. 165.
4. For a full discussion of this case, see L. Nurick and S.J. Schnably, "The First ICSID Conciliation: Tesoro Petroleum Corporation v. Trinidad and Tobago," 1 *ICSID REVIEW—Foreign Investment Law Journal* (1986), pp. 340–353.
5. See generally, Bruce Wolpe and Bertram Levine, *Lobbying Congress: How the System Works* (Washington, D.C.: Congressional Quarterly Press, 1996).

Chapter 8

1. Testimony before the House Foreign Affairs Committee, December 8, 1986, quoted in Bruce C. Wolper and Bertram J. Levine, *Lobbying Congress: How the System Works* (Washington, D.C.: Congressional Quarterly Inc., 2nd ed., 1996), p. 41.
2. Karl Llewellyn, "What Price Contract? An Essay in Perspective," 40 *Yale Law Journal* (1931), pp. 704–751.
3. E. A. Farnsworth, "Precontractual Liability and Preliminary Agreements: Fair Dealing and Failed Negotiation," 87 *Columbia Law Review* (1987), pp. 217–294.
4. S. Litvinoff, "Good Faith," 87 *Tulane Law Review* (1987), pp. 1645–1674.
5. According to one recent case from a U.S. Federal District Court, "the critical inquiry in evaluating the enforceability of an express or implied agreement to negotiate in good faith is whether the standard against which the parties' good-faith negotiations are to be measured is sufficiently certain to comport with the applicable body of contract law." (Howtek, Inc. v. Relisys, et al. 1999. 958 F. Supp. 46 (D.N.H.)

6. J.W. Carter, "The Renegotiation of Contracts," 13 *Journal of Contract Law* (1999), pp. 185–198.
7. Llewellyn, op. cit., pp. 736–737.
8. Wolfgang Peter, *Arbitration and Renegotiation in International Investment Agreements* (London: Kluwer Law International, 1995), p. 79.
9. J. Carver and H. Hossain, "An arbitration case: The dispute that never was," 5 *ICSID Review* (1990), pp. 311–325.
10. Raymond Vernon, *Sovereignty at Bay: The International Spread of U. S. Enterprises* (1971), p. 46.
11. For background on this case, see Richard P. Teisch and William Stoever, "Enron in India: Lessons from a Renegotiation," 35 *Mid-Atlantic Journal of Business* (1999), pp. 51–62.

Chapter 9

1. François de Callières, *De La Manière de négocier avec les souverains. De l'utilité des négociations, du choix des ambassadeurs et des envoyés et des qualitiés nécessaires pour réussir dans ces emplois* (Amsterdam: Pour la Compagnie, 1716). The book has been published in many languages since it was written. The most recent English language version is Francois de Callières, *On the Manner of Negotiating with Princes*, trans. A. F. Whyte, with introduction by Charles Handy (New York: Houghton Mifflin, 2000). The quotations in this chapter are from this edition. A recent French version with a useful bibliography is Francois de Callières, *De La Manière de négocier avec les souverains*, ed. Alain Pekar Lempereur (Paris-Cergy: Essec Irene, 2001).
2. Ibid, p. 6.
3. Ibid., p. 6.
4. Ibid., p. 91.
5. Ibid., p. 20.
6. Ibid., p. 12.
7. Ibid., p. 80.
8. Ibid., p. 25.
9. Ibid., p. 24.
10. Ibid., p. 95.
11. Ibid., p. 82.
12. Ibid., p. 77.
13. Ibid., p. 46.
14. Ibid., p. 82.

Index

access, *see* government access
advisors, as third parties, 154
agents
   mandate of, 50–51
   negotiators as, 47–48
agreements, *see* contracts; draft agreements
Akhromeyev, Sergei, 141–142
Alexander, Jane, 29, 96
alliances, as negotiator's resource, 153
AOL-Time Warner deal, 84
Arab-Israeli conflict, 1991 Madrid Conference, 65
arbitrators, as third parties, 157
authority, political imperatives of, 108–109
automatic adjustment clauses, 173–174

Baltimore, charter school applications, 95
Barnard, Chester, 79
Bechtel Corporation, and Dabhol Power Project, 112–113, 179
Berkshire Hathaway, 73
Brady, Nicholas, 81, 90
   Salomon Brothers negotiation, 73–75, 81, 87
bribes, tips for handling, 61

Buffett, Warren
   Salomon Brothers negotiation, 73–75, 82, 87
   organizational analysis, 77
   reputation of, 97
bureaucracy
   coordination *vs.* conflict, 80
   learning to navigate, 78–79, 82
bureaucrats, negotiating with, 90–91
Bush, George H. W., 77

career interests, political imperatives of, 109
Cesan, Raul, 31
Chrysler
   negotiation with British government, 40
   negotiation with Daimler-Benz, 57–58
coercion, as negotiator's resource, 150
communication with government
   as negotiation, 9, 11
   as right, 8
compromise in negotiations, 17
constituents
   dependence on, 38–40
   importance of knowing, 40
constraints on governments
   budgetary, 42

205

constraints on governments (*continued*)
  constituents as, 38–40
  legal, 43
  negotiation rules as, 33–38
  political imperatives as, 41–42, 43
consultants, as sources of precedent, 127
contracts, *see also* draft agreements
  adaptation clause, 175
  imperfect, 178
  respect for, 187
  stability of, 169–170
Corcoran, Tommy, 96, 114, 151
Corrigan, Gerald, 73, 81
corruption
  facilitated by accountability, 16
  facilitated by discretion, 16
  facilitated by monopoly, 16
  protecting against, 60
  as risk in negotiation, 15
Corruption Perception Index, 15
credibility, as negotiator's resource, 153
culture, as barrier in relationships, 138–139

Dabhol Power Project
  background, 179–180
  extra-deal renegotiation, 179–182
  political imperatives, 112–113
  public opposition, 180
Daimler-Benz, negotiation with Chrysler, 57–58
de Callières, François, 101, 104, 111, 121
  rules of negotiating, 193–198
discretion in negotiation
  danger of corruption, 14–16
  degree of, 12, 13
  as facilitator of corruption, 16

  interpretation of words, 12
  over procedure, 14
disputes
  delay as tactic in, 102–103
  political considerations in, 103
Dole, Robert, 98
draft agreements
  disadvantages, 130–131
  purposes of, 128–129
  tactical advantages, 129–130
Druyan, Darleen, corruption indictment, 15, 16
Dubai Ports World–P & O deal, 84

Eaton, Robert, 58
Egypt
  breach of contract dispute with, 101–103, 111
  "land for security" negotiation with Israel, 66
employees, as sources of precedent, 127
Enron
  and Dabhol Power Project, 112–113, 179–182
  lack of business relationships in India, 184–185
expertise, as negotiator's resource, 150–152
extra-deal renegotiation, 175–192
  changed circumstances as cause, 178–179
  context of, 175–177
  after deal breakdown, 186–192
  before deal breakdown, 182–186
  imperfect contract as cause, 178
Exxon Mobil, use of third party in negotiation, 147–148

Food and Drug Administration
  Clarinex approval hearing, 31
  monopoly power of, 23–24
Ford Foundation
  negotiation with Sudanese gov-

ernment, 48, 55–57, 119–121, 122
Ford, Gerald, 91
foundation relationships, 187
framing
   defined, 142
   negotiating power of, 142–143
   of renegotiation, 191

Galbraith, John Kenneth, 72
General Electric
   and Dabhol Power Project, 112–113, 179
   Honeywell negotiation, 32, 84
George, Henry, 118
gifts, policy for, 62
government
   ability to mobilize popular support, 28
   access to, *see* government access
   challenging authority of, 31
   de Callières' rules for negotiating with, 193–198
   dependence on constituents, 38–40
   as "ghost negotiator," 2
   immunity of, 26–27
   organizational analysis, 76–78
   physical manifestations, 75–76
   power of acting in public interest, 27–29
   power of monopoly, 23–26
   power of privilege, 26–27
   power of protocol, 29–32
   response to political imperatives, 41
   right to communicate with, 8
   rules for influencing, 144
   securing permits from, 3
   self-serving intervention by, 84
   special powers of, 21–22
government access
   constraints on, 33–43
   making the right contact, 87
   by relationship, 95–97
   by reputation, 97–98
   resources as means of, 98
   by right, 94
   rules for gaining, 99–100
Gutfreund, John, and Salomon Brothers cover-up, 75, 115

implicit minor renegotiation clause, 172–173
India, *see* Dabhol Power Project
information, as negotiator's resource, 150–152
interests, *see* political interests
intra-deal renegotiation, 163–164, 169–175
   Asian *vs.* western attitudes, 170–171
   types of clauses, 172–175
   open term provisions, 174
   reluctance to use, 170

Kennedy, Joseph P., 114
Kissinger, Henry, 98
Klitgaard, Robert, 16

legitimacy, as negotiator's resource, 153
Llewellyn, Karl, 162, 172
lobbyists
   expertise of, 150–152
   primary functions of, 151, 155
   relationships as key, 96
   as third parties, 155

Maharashtra State Electricity Board (MSEB), and Dabhol Power Project, 179–182
Maharashtra, state of
   Dabhol Power Project negotiation, 179–180
   renegotiation of deal, 182
   suit to invalidate arbitration clause, 181
mandate
   by internal negotiation, 50

mandate (*continued*)
　securing of, 49–50
　temporary nature of, 51
mediators, as third parties, 157
Medicare drug benefits negotiation, 6
Meir, Golda, 140
Monti, Mario, 32

negotiated decisions, 17
negotiated rulemaking, 9–10
negotiating power
　defined, 118–119
　of framing, 142–143
　of "no surprises," 133–134
　of precedent, 121–127
　of prenegotiations, 134–137
　of relationships, 137–142
　of written materials, 127–133
negotiation
　about rules, 36
　to achieve transactions, 7
　bilateral and multilateral, 6
　de Callières' rules, 193–198
　defined, 11, 104
　discretion in, 12–16
　enlisting help of other governments, 27
　fairness as goal, 35
　interests as key, 104–106
　with monopoly provider, 23–26
　opening moves, 56, 92–93
　participants in, 2–7
　personal dimensions in, 75
　prenegotiation, *see* prenegotiation
　preparing for, *see* preparation for negotiation
　purposes of, 7–10
　vs. renegotiation, 164–165
　rules for, 8–10, 33–38, 44–45
　secrets of, 20
　standards used in, 124
　as team effort, 52–55
　three-phase model, 64–67

negotiation process, 10–17
　conceptualization, 65–66
　detail arrangements, 67
　phases of, 34–36
　prenegotiation, *see* prenegotiation
　rules of, 33–38
　sealed bidding process, 34
negotiation team
　advance preparation, 53
　allocation of functions, 54
　selection of, 54–55
　single spokesperson for, 54
negotiators
　as agents, 47–48
　"architects" *vs.* "good soldiers," 51–52
　assets used by, 149–153
　classes of, 88–91
　as organizational representatives, 74
Northwest Airlines(KLM negotiations, 70

open term provisions, 174

Pfizer, political contributions, 97
pharmaceutical industry, lobbying against price discounts, 6
political appointees, negotiating with, 89–90
political contributions, to gain access, 97
political imperatives
　accepting blame, 114–116
　finding alternate resources, 113–114
　giving credit, 114–115
　intensity of, 110
　involving third parties, 111–113
　in negotiation, 107–110
　shifting request to different department, 116
　strategies for coping, 111–116

political interests
 of constituents, 108
 importance in negotiation, 104–106
 rules for dealing with, 116
 separate entities of, 106–107
 types of, 108–110
politicians, negotiating with, 88
post-deal renegotiation, 165–169
 contractual constraints, 166
 distinguishing factors, 165–167
 obligation for, 166
 process guidelines, 167–169
power, *see* negotiating power
precedent
 in absence of rules, 123
 finding the right, 125–127
 historical, 125
 need for relevance, 126
 need for specificity, 126
 negotiating power of, 121–124
 as protection against opponents, 123–124
 sources of, 127
prenegotiation, 65–66
 building relationships, 68
 consulting key players, 69–70
 developing alliances, 68
 informing the public, 68–69
 power of, 134–137
 preparing the environment, 70
 rules for, 71
 setting an agenda, 70
 steps, 135
preparation for negotiation
 defining one's interests, 58–60
 determining goals, 47–48
 determining options, 57–58
 exploring internal interests, 49
 formulating advance proposals, 63–64
 identifying key issues, 62–63
 importance of, 46–47
 need for mandate, 49–52

 researching counterparts, 55–57
 selecting the team, 52–55
Prince, Charles, accepting responsibility for Citigroup actions, 115–116
procurement rules, 33
protocol, rules used to influence and intimidate, 29–30

Raytheon, negotiating with NATO and Japan, 39
Reagan, Ronald, 21
Reebok, 145–146, 158–159
relationships
 as key for lobbyists, 96
 as key in avoiding renegotiation, 183
 negotiating power of, 137–142
 as negotiator's resource, 152
 sharing experiences, 140–141
 showing interest in other side, 139–140
 steps in building, 139–142
 "two cultures" as barrier, 138–139
renegotiation
 appropriate process, 190–191
 clauses, 174–175
 creating value in, 188–189
 defined, 163
 demand for, 188
 English common law view of, 176
 extra-deal, 164, 175–192
 framing of, 191
 intra-deal, 163–164, 169–175
 involving secondary parties, 190
 litigation as alternative, 189
 mediator's role in, 191–192
 vs. negotiation, 164–165
 post-deal, 163, 165–169
 risk of, 162
 rules for, 192
review clauses, 173
rewards, as resource, 149–150

Rickover, Hyman, 32
right of petition, protected by U.S. Constitution, 8
Roosevelt, Franklin D., 37, 96

Sadat, Anwar, 37
Salomon Brothers *vs.* U.S. Treasury Department, 72–75
Sarbanes-Oxley Act, 36
Schrempp, Jürgen, 57–58
Shakespeare, William, 145
Shering-Plough, Clarinex approval hearing, 31
Shultz, George, 141–142, 161, 162
Snow, C. P., 139
standards in negotiation, 124
St. Lawrence Cement Company
  negotiations to build new plant, 6
  opening moves, 92–93
  political constraints, 31
  public opposition, 63
Stockton, Frank, 56
Sudanese government, negotiations with, 55–57, 120–121, 122, 134, 143
surprises, avoiding in negotiations, 133–134

Taghkanic, NY, Zoning Board of Appeals, discretion used by, 13
team, *see* negotiation team
Tennessee Valley Authority (TVA), explicit *vs.* implied authorization, 37
Tesoro Petroleum Company, negotiation with Trinidad and Tobago, 151–152
The Lady and the Tiger, 56

third parties
  effectiveness of, 146–147
  need for, 149–154
  roles of, 154–157, 186
  selection of, 159
third-party intervention
  cost of, 158–159
  in negotiations, 5, 147–148
  rules for, 159–160
  strategy, 148–149
Transparency International, 15
Trinidad and Tobago, negotiation with Tesoro Petroleum, 151–152
Tufts University, failure to prenegotiate, 135

U.S. Air Force, procurement corruption case, 15, 16
U.S. Foreign Corrupt Practices Act, 60

Visiting Nurses Association, failure to prenegotiate, 135–136

Weber, Max, 79
Welch, Jack, 32
Wilberforce, Lord, 152, 157
Wilson, James Q., 79
World Bank
  role in international investment disputes, 102
  as third party in negotiation, 147–148
written materials
  draft agreements, 128–131
  negotiating power of, 127–133
  rules for use of, 132–133
  standard form contracts, 128

zoning ordinances, customary accessory use in, 13

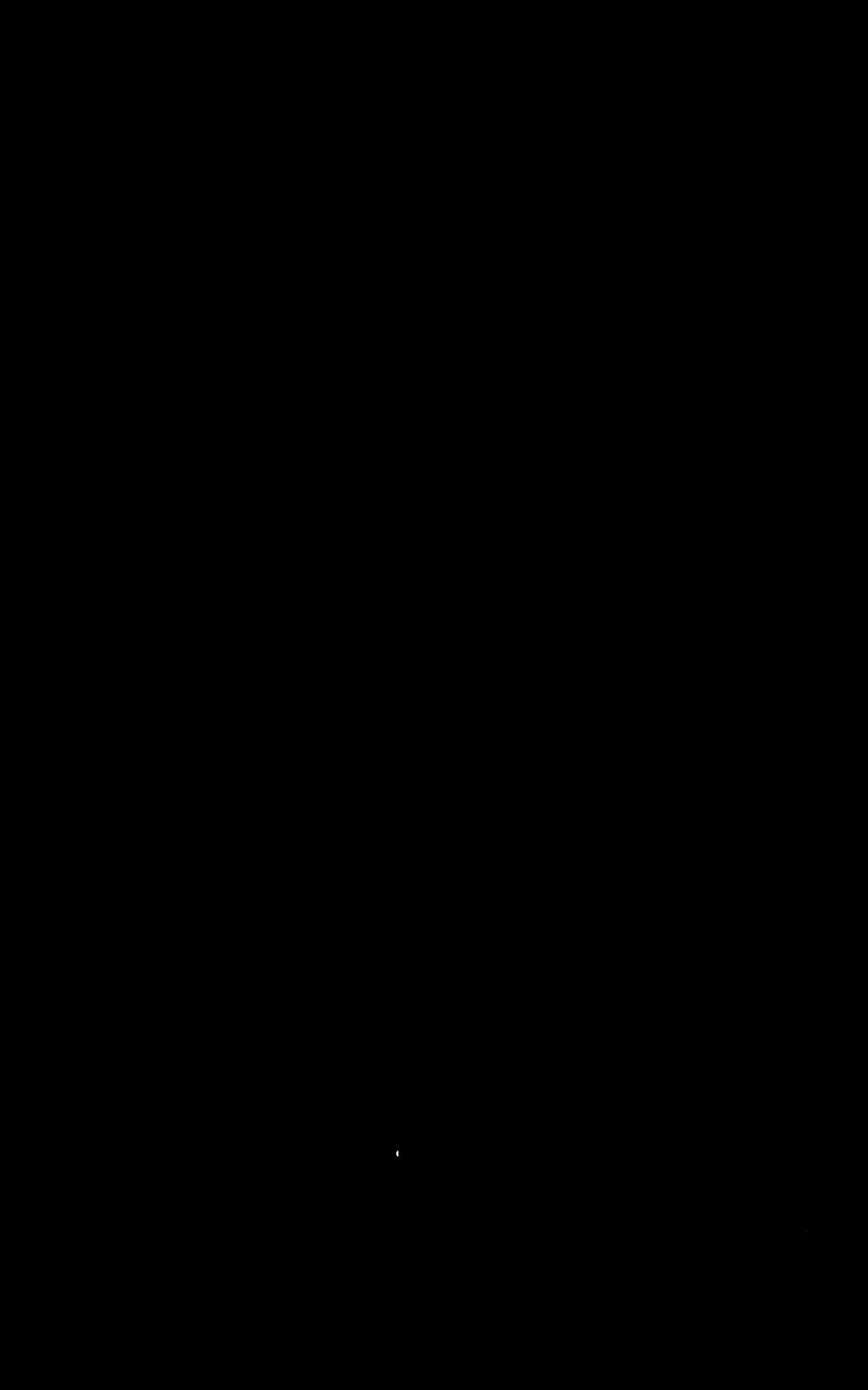

HD 58.6 .S257 2008
Salacuse, Jeswald W.
Seven secrets for
 negotiating with government

JAN 3 0 2008